This book has been published by the Museu d'Art Contemporani de Barcelona on the occasion of the exhibition *Gerhard Richter. Atlas* (April 23-July 4, 1999). Some of these texts have been already published. We thank the authors for their kind permission to publish these essays, as well as for their collaboration in revising and bringing them up to date.

Selection of texts
Manuel J. Borja-Villel
José Lebrero Stals

Coordination
Anna Jiménez Jorquera
Elisabet Surís

Graphic Design
Toni Miserachs

Typesetting and realization
Eumo Gràfic

Translations
Steven S. Lindberg
Stephen Wright

Printing
Romanyà/Valls s.a.

DL. B-14.907-00
ISBN: 84-89771-91-X

2nd edition: 2000

Museu d'Art Contemporani de Barcelona
Plaça dels Àngels, 1. 08001 Barcelona

EXHIBITION

Curatorship
Manuel J. Borja-Villel
José Lebrero Stals

Coordination
Anna Borrell

Assistant to coordination
Emma Gajo

Realization
Isabel Bachs; Croquis

Public Programs
Josep M. Muñoz

Activities
Anna Guarro
Yolanda Nicolás

Educational Programs
Antònia M. Cerdà

Communication
Nicola Wohlfarth

Supporting Members of MACBA
Fundación Andersen Consulting
Port de Barcelona
Carlos Duran

B. H.D. Buchloh / J. F. Chevrier / A. Zweite / R. Rochlitz

PHOTOGRAPHY AND PAINTING IN THE WORK OF GERHARD RICHTER

Four essays on *Atlas*

LLIBRES DE RECERCA

B. H.D. Buchloh / J. F. Chevrier / A. Zweite / R. Rochlitz

PHOTOGRAPHY AND PAINTING IN THE WORK OF GERHARD RICHTER

Four essays on *Atlas*

MAC BA Museu d'Art Contemporani de Barcelona

CONTENTS

Preface 9

Gerhard Richter's Atlas:
The Anomic Archive
Benjamin H.D. Buchloh 11

Between the Fine Arts and the Media
(The German example: Gerhard Richter)
Jean-François Chevrier 31

Gerhard Richter's «Album of
Photographs, Collages, and Sketches»
Armin Zweite 61

«Where we have got to»
Rainer Rochlitz 103

Illustrations 126

PREFACE

The present publication, which brings together four perspectives for the analysis of the complex and determining role played by the photographic image in the pictorial work of Gerhard Richter, coincides with the exhibition *Gerhard Richter. Atlas* at the MACBA from the 23 of April to the 4 of July 1999. In addition to the compendium *Atlas*, this exhibition includes a selection of twenty-two paintings which span more than three decades of the artist's work.

The realization of this project would not have been possible without the co-operation and the generosity of numerous individuals and institutions, both public and private, to all of whom we wish to express our gratitude for their decisive contribution: to the Städtische Galerie im Lenbachhaus in Munich, of whose collection *Atlas* forms a part, and to its director Helmut Friedel, assisted by Ulrich Wilmes and Susanne Boeller; to Massimo Martino in Mendrisio; to the Institut d'art contemporain Frac Rhône-Alpes in Villeurbanne and to its director Yannick Miloux; to the Sammlung Frieder Burda; to the Kunstsammlung Nordrhein-Westfalen in Düsseldorf and to its director Armin Zweite; to the Museum für Moderne Kunst in Frankfurt; to the Centre Georges Pompidou, Musée national d'art moderne/Centre de création industrielle in Paris; to Fred Jahn in Munich; to the Kunstmuseum Winterthur; to the Musée départemental d'art contemporain in Rochechouart; to the Museum Boijmans van Beuningen in Rotterdam; to the Anthony d'Offay Gallery in London; to the galleries Marian Goodman and Luhring Augustine in New York; to Frank Wickert, the artist's assistant; to all those lenders who have preferred to remain anonymous, and finally to Gerhard Richter, who worked with us throughout the entire process, contributing his critical comments to the project.

GERHARD RICHTER'S *ATLAS*: THE ANOMIC ARCHIVE

Benjamin H.D. Buchloh

What photographs by their sheer accumulation attempt to banish is the collection of death, which is part and parcel of every memory image. In the illustrated magazines the world has become a photographable present and the photographed present has been entirely eternalized. Seemingly ripped from the clutch of death, in reality it has succumbed to it.

In the exact duplication of the Real, preferably by means of another reproductive medium—advertisement, photography, etc.—and in the shift from medium to medium, the real vanishes and becomes an allegory of death. But even in its moment of destruction it exposes and affirms itself, it will become the quintessential real and it becomes the fetishism of the lost object.

Gerhard Richter's *Atlas*, is one of several structurally similar, yet rather different projects by a number of European artists from the early to mid 1960s whose formal procedures of accumulating found or intentionally produced photographs in more or less regular grid formations have remained enigmatic (one could also think of the forty year-old collection of typologies of industrial architecture by Bernhard and Hilla Becher begun in 1958 or the work of Christian Boltanski begun in the late 1960s). They are either notable for their astonishing homogeneity and continuity (as is the case with the work of the Bechers) or for the equally remarkable heterogeneity and discontinuity that defines Richter's *Atlas*. Having made photography's innate structural order of the archive, its seemingly infinite multiplicity, serialization and aim for comprehensive totality the principles of the work's formal organization, these projects share first of all a condition of not being classifiable within the typology and terminology of avant-garde art history: neither the term «collage» nor the term «photomontage» would adequately describe the apparent formal and iconographic monotony of these panels, the vast archival accumulations of their materials. Yet at the same time, the descriptive terms and genres from the more specialized history of photography, all of them operative in one way or the other in Richter's *Atlas*, appear equally inadequate to classify these image accumulations.

Despite the first impression that the *Atlas* might provide, neither the private album of the amateur, nor the cumulative projects of documentary photography could identify the discursive order of this photographic collection. And we could not argue either that the exactitude of topographical or architectural photography or the massive image apparatus of surveillance and spectacularization operative in photojournalism govern the peculiar «photographic condition» of Richter's *Atlas*. Lastly, in spite of their frequent appearance among the genres presented, not even advertisement and fashion photography and its principles of fetishization determine the reading of these panels. By contrast, what could come to mind first of all are the terms with which one would describe instructive charts, teaching devices, technical or scientific illustrations found in textbooks or catalogues, the archival organization of materials according to the principles of a still unidentifiable discipline. Avant-garde history, however, seems to have few if any precedents for artistic procedures that organize knowledge systematically within didactic models of display or as mnemonic devices. If such precedents do appear—as for example in the teaching panels produced by Kasimir Malevich between 1924 and 1927 which illustrate the theoretical efforts of the Institute of Artistic Culture in Leningrad—they are generally considered as mere supplements to the actual aesthetic objects. This would also be the case with another crucial example that has similarly remained outside of the historian's terminological purview, Hannah Höch's

Media Scrap Book, which the artist produced around 1933. Höch's project points distinctly towards the earlier existence of a variety of artistic strategies which attempt to organize and accommodate large quantities of found photographs in an archival manner. Rather than deploying fragmentation and fissure as the dynamic principles of photomontage that Höch had practiced in the late 1910s, her turn towards the foregrounding of photography's archival order seems to be probing the subject's continuing mnemonic competence in the face of rising media culture. The tracing of historical processes, the establishment of typologies, chronologies and temporal continuities—even if only fictitious, as in Boltanski's case—seem to have conflicted for the longest time with the avant-garde's self perception as providing instantaneous presence, shock and perceptual rupture.

Excursus on the *Atlas*

The term «Atlas» rings perhaps more familiar in the German language than it does in English, being defined since the end of the sixteenth century as a book format that compiles and organizes geographical and astronomical knowledge. We are told that this format received its name from one of Mercator's map collections in 1585 which carried a frontispiece showing an image of Atlas, the titan of Greek mythology who holds up the universe at the threshold where day and night meet each other. But later, in the nineteenth century, the term had been increasingly deployed to identify any tabular display of systematized knowledge and one could have encountered an atlas in almost all fields of the empirical sciences: an atlas of astronomy, of anatomy, geography and ethnography, and later even schoolbooks charted plants and animals and bore that name like the titan who held up the heavens. When the confidence in empiricism and the aspiration towards comprehensive completeness of positivist systems of knowledge withered in the twentieth century, the term «Atlas» seems to have fallen into a more metaphorical usage.

Aby Warburg's *Mnemosyne Atlas*

Thus we encounter the most important example of this tendency around 1927 in a monumental project which sets out to gather identifiable forms of collective memory: the *Mnemosyne Atlas* was first conceived by the art historian Aby Warburg in 1925 after his release from Ludwig Binswanger's psychiatric clinic in 1924; actively developed in 1928, it was continued until his death in 1929. Even though the scholar had to leave the project in an unfinished state, more than sixty panels with over one thousand photographs had been assembled by Warburg at the time of his death. According to his aspirations as recorded in the diaries, the *Mnemosyne Atlas* sought to construct a model of the mnemonic in which Western European humanist thought would once more, perhaps for the last time, recognize its origins and trace its latent continuities into the present, ranging spatially across the confines of European humanist culture and situating itself temporally within the parameters of European history from classical antiquity to the present.

While according to Warburg collective social memory could be traced through the various layers of cultural transmission (his primary focus being the transformation of «dynamograms» transferred from classical antiquity to Renaissance painting, the reoccurring motifs of gesture and bodily expression that he had identified in his notorious term as «*pathos* formulas»), Warburg more specifically argued that his attempt to construct collective historical memory would focus on the inextricable link between the mnemonic and the traumatic. Thus he wrote in the unpublished introduction to his *Mnemosyne Atlas* that it is in the area of orgiastic mass seizure that one should look for the mint that stamps the expression of extreme emotional seizure on the memory with such intensity that the engrams of that experience of suffering live on, an inheritence preserved in the memory.

While this introduction to the project reads retrospectively like an uncanny prognosis of the imminent future of social behaviour, Warburg evidently hoped to construct—even if for the last time—a model of historical memory and continuity of experience, before both were shattered by the catastrophic destruction of humanist civilization at the hands of German Fascism. But the *Atlas*, at least according to its author's intentions, would also accomplish a materialist project of constructing social memory by collecting photographic reproductions of a broad variety of practices of representation. Warburg's *Atlas* thus not only reiterated first of all his life-long challenge to the rigorous and hierarchical compartmentalization of the discipline of art history, by attempting to abolish its methods and categories of exclusively formal or stylistic description. Yet by eroding the disciplinary boundaries between the conventions and the studies of high art and mass culture, the *Atlas* also questioned whether mnemonic experience could even be constructed any longer under the universal reign of photographic reproduction, establishing the theoretical and the presentational framework to probe the competence of the mnemonic from which Höch's scrapbook would emerge a few years later.

Kurt Forster, the editor of the forthcoming English edition of Warburg's writings, describes the arrangement as follows:

> There, cheek by jowl, were late antique reliefs, secular manuscripts, monumental frescoes, postage stamps, broadsides, pictures cut out of magazines, and old master drawings. It becomes apparent, if only at second glance, that this unorthodox selection is the product of an extraordinary command of a vast field.

It seems, at least at first reading, that we encounter in Warburg's project an almost Benjaminian trust in the universally emancipatory functions of technological reproduction and dissemination. Thus, the extreme temporal and spatial heterogeneity of the *Atlas*'s subjects is juxtaposed with the paradoxical homogeneity of their simultaneous presence in the space of the photographic, anticipating the subsequent abstraction from historical context and social function in the name of a universal aesthetic experience by André Malraux in his *Le Musée imaginaire*. This condition alone seems at first sight—at least—to situate the *Mnemosyne Atlas* also in a peculiar parallelism to artistic practices of the historic avant-garde of the 1920s. Not surprisingly, this argument has is in fact been made by numerous Warburg scholars, notably by Wolfgang Kemp, Werner Hofmann and most recently and most emphatically by Forster himself in his two essays on Warburg's methods. Forster states, for example, that in terms of technique Warburg's panels belong with the montage procedures of Schwitters and Lissitzky. Needless to say, this analogy implies no claim to artistic merit on the part of the Warburg panels; nor does it invalidate that of Schwitters' and Lissitzky's collages: it simply serves to redefine graphic montage as the construction of meanings rather than the arrangement of forms.

It is this remark (and many similar ones by the Warburg scholars mentioned), in particular its intriguing and surprisingly clear-cut opposition between a «construction of meanings» (supposedly Warburg's) and an «arrangement of forms» (supposedly that of Kurt Schwitters and El Lissitzky) which poses another question. First of all, whether any aspects of Warburg's *Atlas* can in fact be productively compared to the collage and photomontage techniques of the 1920's or whether we could understand more about either side of this problematic comparison by differentiating its two parts more rigorously and—most importantly for our project—by recognizing that the *Atlas* in fact established a cultural model of probing the possibilities of historical memory whose agenda was profoundly different from its activist precursors in the field of photomontage. Second ther is the question, whether it could in fact be potentially productive to compare Warburg's *Atlas* with Richter's *Atlas*, as another example of such a mnemonic project. We would have to recognize first of all that while both projects obviously address the possibilities of mnemonic experience, they operate under dramatically different historical circumstances: the former at the onset of a traumatic destruction of historical memory, the moment of the most devastating cataclysm of human history brought about by German Fascism, the latter looking back at its aftermath from a position of repression and disavowal, attempting to reconstruct remembrance from within the social and geo-political space of the society that inflicted trauma.

Structures of an Atlas

Wolfgang Kemp was the first to point out that Warburg's project of an organization and presentation of vast quantities of historical information without any textual commentary should remind us of Surrealist montage procedures. Thereby, Warburg's *Atlas* inevitably enters also into a comparison with another extraordinary and unfinished montage-project of the late 1920s, a textual assemblage which had attempted to construct an analytical memory of collective experience in nineteenth century Paris. Benjamin had equally associated his *Passagenwerk* with the montage techniques of the Surrealists and had explicitly identified it in those terms when he wrote that the «method of this work is literary montage. I have nothing to say, only to show.»

And Theodor W. Adorno's description of the *Passagenwerk* could just as well be applied to the essential features of Warburg's *Mnemosyne Atlas*:

> ... (Benjamin) deliberately excluded all interpretation and wanted the actually existing conditions to be foregrounded through the shocks that the montage of the materials would inevitably generate in the reader... To bring his antisubjectivism to the point of culmination, Benjamin envisaged that the work should only consist of accumulated quotations.

Again, several terms stand out in this discussion that deserve our attention, with regard to both the accuracy of the description of (and the potential differences between) Benjamin's and Warburg's model and to the accuracy of their definition of the epistemes of collage/photomontage and the question whether these are in fact the epistemes of the structural organization of the *Atlas*: first of all, the exclusion of interpretation in favor of actually existing conditions in the discursive construction of the textual memory. Second: the anticipation of shocks as an inescapable and intended result of the montage technique, presumably occurring most vividly in the interstices of discursive fields (such as the pictorial versus the photographic, the mass-cultural clutter versus the structural distillation of the avant-garde strategy, the artisanal versus the technically reproduced, the textual versus the painterly: to name but a few of the classical *topoi* and tropes of collage and montage aesthetics).

Thirdly, and crucially, it is Adorno's observation of antisubjectivism as the driving force of the collage/photomontage aesthetic that presumably articulates a systematic critique of what would later come to be called «the author function» of a text. And lastly, and directly connected with the preceding term, Adorno's emphasis on the accumulation of quotations as a newly emerging structuring device of montage aesthetics: first of all, in photo-montage itself where it displaces the homogeneity of the conception and execution of painting. But soon thereafter, montage was also to transform literary or filmic aesthetics (those of the Soviet Union in particular) as for example in the factographic novel where it will displace authorial omniscience, narrative and fiction.

Thus one could argue that by the mid 1920s a variety of homologous new models of writing and imaging historical accounts emerged simultaneously, ranging from the montage techniques of artistic practices to Warburg's *Atlas* or those of the *Annales* historians. In all of these projects (literary, artistic, filmic, historical) a post-humanist and post-bourgeois subjectivity is constituted. The telling of history as a sequence of events and accounts of its individual agents is displaced by a focus on the simultaneity of separate but contingent social frameworks and an infinity of participating agents, while the process of history is reconceived as a structural system of perpetually changing interactions and permutations between economic and ecological givens, class formations and their ideologies, and the resulting types of social and cultural interactions specific to each particular moment.

Even if Warburg's *Atlas* was in fact part of a newly emerging cultural paradigm of montage as a new process of writing a decentered history and constructing mnemonic forms accordingly, any comparison between Warburg and the montage techniques of the artistic avant-gardes, let alone the neo-avant-garde, will remain highly problematic if it does not recognize first of all the actual discontinuities of the collage/photomontage model itself. These internal shifts and breaks in the paradigm emerge already in the late 1920s, and these changes were to become especially decisive in the paradigm's rediscovery in post-war practices. Furthermore, any attempt at a comparative reading of the structurally comparable projects will have to develop an equally differentiated understanding of the contradictions and changes which emerge already in the 1920s in the definitions of photographic functions themselves, as much in the theoretical approaches to photography in Weimar Germany and the Soviet Union as in the artistic practices deploying photography in both countries. More specifically, and particularly important for our discussion of Warburg's and Richter's mnemonic project, is the fact that at the very moment of its elaboration, opposite theorizations of photography had collided precisely on the question of the impact of the photographic image on the construction of historical memory.

This dialectic is evident in the positions articulated in 1927-1928: on the one hand we have to consider Siegfried Kracauer's epochal essay on photography arguing that photographic production devastates the memory image, a position which implies (most likely unbeknown to both) a severe criticial challenge of Warburg's project to conceive of the *Atlas* as a model of the construction of social memory. At the opposite end of the spectrum one would have to consider the famous «photography debate» of the Soviet Union as it emerges equally around 1927, primarily in the writings of the Soviet theorists and artists Ossip Brik, Boris Kushner and Alexander Rodchenko. And thirdly one would have to consider what remains probably the most important essay on photography of the first half of the twentieth century, written shortly after Warburg's project was interrupted: Walter Benjamin's *Short History of Photography* of 1931, which argues against the media pessimism of Kracauer's essay in favour of a new media culture of politically motivated montage.

To sketch out these oppositions only in the briefest terms we will would have to point first of all to the latent dichotomy operative in collage/montage aesthetics from their inception: the poles of opposition could be called the order of perceptual shock and the principle of estrangement on the one side, and the order of the statistical collection or the order of the archive on the other. The structural emphasis on discontinuity and fragmentation in the initial phase of Dada-derived photomontage introduced the subject's perceptual field to the «shock» experiences of daily existence in advanced industrial culture. While the metonymic procedures of photomontage and their continuous emphasis on the fissure and the fragment—at least in their initial appearance—operated to dismantle the myths of unity and totality that advertising and ideology consistently inscribe on their consumers, photomontage paradoxically collaborated also in the social project of perceptual modernization and its affirmative agenda. But this revolutionary effect of the semiotic upheaval of poetic shock and estrangement was short-lived. Already in the second moment of Dada collage (at the time of Hannah Höch's *Meine Haussprüche*, 1922) for example, the heterogeneity of random order and the arbitrary juxtapositions of found objects and images, and the sense of a fundamental cognitive and perceptual anomie, were challenged as either apolitical and anti-communicative, or as esoteric and aestheticist. The very avant-garde artists who initiated photomontage (e.g. Heartfield and Höch, Klucis, Lissitzky, Rodchenko) now diagnosed this anomic character of the Dada-collage/montage technique as bourgeois avant-gardism, mounting a critique that called, paradoxically, for a reintroduction of the dimensions of narrative, communicative action and instrumentalized logic within the structural organization of montage aesthetics.

What we are witnessing in fact, first in the mid-1920's and, becoming more decisive in the later 1920's, is precisely a gradual shift towards the order of the archival and mnemonic functions of the photographic collection as the underlying episteme of a radically different aesthetics of photomontage. In terms of its conception of the photographic, it is a shift that originates in the same confidence in photography's versatility and reliability that was also to drive Warburg's archival project and his confidence in the photograph's authenticity as empirical document, and the radical emancipatory power of the egalitarian effects of photographic reproduction. The photographic image in general was now defined as dynamic, contextual and contingent, and the serial structuring of visual information emphasized open form and a potential infinity, not only of photographic subjects eligible in a new social collective but equally an infinity of contingent, photographically recordable details and facets that would constitute each individual subject within perpetually altered activities, social relations and object relationships. Once again it would be worthwhile to investigate the parallels of the Soviet model of the photographic with the radical reconception of the historical process emerging simultaneously in the work of the French *Annales* historians Marc Bloch and Lucien Febvre. These parallels between the conception of the historical process and the construction and ordering of the photographic representation become most obvious, then, when we read Ossip Brik's argument suggesting:

> ... to differentiate individual objects so as to make a pictorial record of them is not only a technical but also an ideological phenomenon. In the pre-Revolutionary (feudal and bourgeois) period, both painting and literature set themselves the aim of differentiating individual people and events from their general context and concentrating attention on them... To the contemporary consciousness, an individual person can be understood and assessed only in connection with all the other people—with those who used to be regarded by the pre-revolutionary consciousness as background.

This argument implies a radical redefinition of the photographic object itself. It is no longer conceived as a single-image print, carefully crafted by the artist-photographer in the studio, framed and presented as a pictorial substitute. Rather, as was the case already for Rodchenko's definition, it is precisely the cheaply and rapidly produced snapshot that will displace the traditional synthetic portrait. The organizational and distributional form will now become the archive, or as Rodchenko called it, the photo-file, a loosely organized, more or less coherent accumulation of snapshots relating and documenting one particular subject.

Instead of plotting the future models of participatory photographic experience under Socialism, Siegfried Kracauer analyzed the actually existing usages of the photographic image in the Capitalist media practices of Weimar Germany, specifically those governing the illustrated weeklies. Linking the capacity of the formation of memory images to an actual relationship with material and cognitive objects, Kracauer's extreme media pessimism recognizes that it is precisely the universal presence of the photographic image that will eventually destroy cognitive and mnemonic processes altogether. Thus he argues:

> Never before has an age been so informed about itself, if being informed means having an image of objects that resembles them in a photographic sense. [...] In reality, however, the weekly photographic ration does not at all mean to refer to these objects or *ur-images*. If it were offering itself as an aid to memory, then memory would have to make the selection. But the flood of photos sweeps away the dams of memory. The assault of this mass of images is so powerful that it threatens to destroy the potentially existing awareness of crucial traits. Artworks suffer this fate through their reproductions. [...] In the illustrated magazines people see the very world that the illustrated magazines prevent them from perceiving. [...] Never before has a period known so little about itself.

This was the moment when the rise of a photographic media culture allowed a first insight into the newly emerging collective conditions of anomie, the moment when it became possible to imagine that mass cultural representation would cause the destruction of mnemonic experience and of historical thought altogether. Therefore, one of the most enigmatic—and with hindsight ever more plausible—arguments made by Benjamin in 1931 suggested that the historical climax of the medium of photography might have to be situated around 1860, since the photograph at that moment had barely accomplished the transition from the auratic object to the increasingly emptied structure of mere technological reproduction and at the same time, photography—as an emerging emancipatory technology—could still contain the social promise of radically different forms of collective interaction and subject-hood.

The Beginnings of Richter's *Atlas*

If we now consider how the works of artists of the post war period, and Richter's *Atlas* in particular, positioned themselves with regard to these photographic legacies of the historical avant-gardes, we can easily recognize that Richter's collection of found amateur photographs, of journalistic and advertisement photography, inverts the utopian aspirations of the avant-garde on every level: if some of the Soviet and Weimar practices and theorizations had defined photography in a teleological perspective as a cultural project of enactment and empowerment, of articulation and of self-determination, Richter contemplates the reigning social usages of photography and their potential artistic functions from the outset with an attitude of profound scepticism. If the agitational and emancipatory dimension of photomontage had originated in a desire for the radical transformation of hierarchical class relations and of the structures that determine authorship and production, Richter's *Atlas* seems to consider photography and its various practices as a system of ideological domination and more precisely as one of the instruments with which collective anomie, amnesia and repression are socially inscribed.

After his transition from East to West Germany in 1961, Richter started this collection of photographic images whose ultimate purpose—at least initially—seems to have been unclear even to him: organized according to the most traditional display system of a rectangular grid, the images—at first glance at least—appear to have been chosen solely for their sentimental value of recording instances and subjects from family history. Only one of the images from the first four panels would later serve as a matrix for one of Richter's photopaintings, begun at the time when the initial panels for the *Atlas* were assembled (*Christa und Wolfi*, 1964). The others—including the third panel, consisting almost entirely of amateur landscape photographs taken on holiday trips—would remain seemingly mute, inconsequential documents. These photographic images appear at first as though they had been torn out of the family album shortly before Richter's flight from East Germany, to serve as souvenirs of a past that was being left behind forever, or as though they might have been mailed to him from his relatives in the East to console the young artist for his recent departure from his loved ones.

If we assume that the initial impulse to form the *Atlas* originated in fact in Richter's recent experience of the loss of a familial and social context, and in the encounter with Germany's self-inflicted destruction of the identity of the nation state, it would be plausible to consider the *Atlas* as one more, and in many ways very different, example in a longstanding tradition of cultural practices, just as Warburg's *Mnemosyne Atlas* on the other side of that historical divide had responded to a similar experience of a particularly acute «memory crisis». But as we indicated earlier, a different type of «memory crisis» had been confronted by artists and by theoreticians of photography already in the late 1920s, prior to the historical destruction of humanist subjectivity, but not to the rise of a photographic mass culture and its devastating (or emancipatory) effects on the auratic work of art and the mnemonic image. Mnemonic desire, it appears then, is activated especially in those moments of extreme duress in which the traditional material bonds between subjects, between subjects and objects, and between objects and their representation appear to be on the verge of displacement, if not outright disappearance. Undoubtedly this would have been a condition foundational to post-war German culture in particular, entangled in the double bind of the collective disavowal of history, the repression of the recent past and an almost hysterically accelerated and expanded apparatus of photographic production to solicit artificial desire and consumption.

It is now one of the difficulties of positioning Richter's *Atlas* within that double perspective, and we have to relate, if not integrate, those two rather different formations within which the work could be conceived as responding to the condition of this dual «memory crisis». The first one is utterly historical and specific to the social and ideological framework of post-war Germany after Fascism. The second, in possible contrast with, but not entirely to the first, considers the impact of photographic media culture on the project of painting and on the conception of authentic object experience at large. Clearly, the questions raised by Kracauer concerned first of all the devastating impact of the photograph on the artisan-produced auratic work of art which contained what he would call the «monogram of history». In Kracauer's enigmatic definition, this «monogram» constituted the singularity of artistic form, in that it succeeded in bringing the knowledge of death to the deepest resolution within the representation and thereby resisted repression at its most profound level.

Richter, as a subject of the post-war period, would now have to rephrase this very question, namely whether it could even be possible to conceive mnemonic images at the moment of the most violent, collectively enacted repression of history, a repression for which photographic media culture had now become, even more than in Kracauer's time, the primary agent. Simultaneously, Richter as a painter would have seen himself—like all other painters of his generation—confronted with the question of whether and how paintings could any longer be conceived at all in the confrontation with the apparatus of photographic mass culture.

The photographic images of family members making up the first four panels of the *Atlas* therefore seem to have served Richter—as they had served for Kracauer in 1927 and Benjamin in 1931 and again for Roland Barthes in 1979 (when the confrontation with the death of his mother made him write a contemporary phenomenology of photography)—as the point from which the reflection on the relationship between photography and historical memory would originate. As though photography's oscillating ambiguity, as a dubious agent simultaneously enacting and destroying mnemonic experience, could at least be fixed for one moment by situating the image in an analogue to the mnemonic imprint of the family relation itself.

After all, this is the imprint where physical contiguity and the referent of psychic inscription could not be questioned, where the causality and materiality of mnemonic experience seemed to be guaranteed. Whether this mnemonic imprint would be defined as that of genetic and hereditary encoding (the foundation of a proto-racist theory as suggested in the theory of memory developed by Aby Warburg's teacher, Richard Semon), or whether it would trace the more or less successful psycho-sexual organization according to the Oedipal laws that determine the formation of subjectivity (e.g. Freud's inherent definition of psychic memory), or whether memory would be conceived of as determined by class and social institution (as proposed in Durckheim's theorization of memory structure): it is in the reflection upon the family image that the power of mnemonic ties to the past and their inextricable impact on the present could be most credibly verified as material processes, alternately—like photography—assuring and assaulting the formation of identity.

The fact that the mobilization of an *Atlas* of remembrance against a massive apparatus of repression did not just result from the private experience of a loss of a geo-political context and social-familial order but, as we have argued, to an equal degree from the encounter with the rapidly changing functions and structures of the photographic image that Richter discovered after his arrival in the West, is already apparent in the fifth panel of the *Atlas* where the homogeneity of the photographic material which had heretofore consisted exclusively of the more or less haphazard collection from the family album is eroded by a peculiar, at first unfathomable, heterogeneity of picture types.

Introducing a variety of clippings from the West German illustrated journals (such as *Der Stern*), Richter seems to have recorded his first encounters with mass cultural genres until then more or less unknown to him. Having escaped from a country where advertising of any kind was prohibited, where fashion photography (let alone soft—or hard—pornography) were outlawed, and where images fuelling the desire for tourist travel and consumption would have been banned from the photographic public sphere of the Communist state, Richter could now, for the first time, endlessly peruse these images in abundance. It is not surprising then to see that precisely those categories (fashion, travel, soft-core pornography and advertisement) did in fact become the first to disperse the homogeneity of the amateur and family photographs of the first four panels of the *Atlas*.

In an almost exact analogy to the beginning of Kracauer's essay, Richter thereby juxtaposes the construction of public identity by media culture with the construction of private identity through the family photograph. Memory is thus conceived of in Richter's *Atlas* first of all as an archaeology of pictorial and photographic registers, each of which partakes in a different photographic formation, and each of which generates its proper psychic register of responses. While all of them operate separately (and in relative independence from each other) in the perceptual and the mnemonic apparatus of the subject, they all intersect, constituting precisely that complex field of disavowals and displacements, the field of repression and cover images within which memory is constituted in the register of the photographic order. What had made Kracauer's observation in the initial paragraphs of his essay so uncanny (in the parallel discussion of the image of the glamorous movie star and the grandmother) was the realization that—with the rise of media culture—the subject would no longer be primarily constituted within the models of continuity that ethnicity and family, nation state and culture, tradition, class and social customs had provided. Not even the bodily site of the mnemonic appeared any longer as a guaranteed referent, encroached upon as it was by the rapidly shifting fashion system. Instead, newly constructed signs and languages, residing and operating outside of all the mnemonic forms of experience that the family figures had represented, would now enter the mnemonic field, binding the desire for identity in different representational registers altogether.

Thus rather abruptly, in Kracauer's first image, the reader/spectator's libidinal investment is reoriented towards a female figure never known and that never will be known other than in the photographic representation. Her body is no longer the site of the auratic presence of lived experience and lived encounters (like that of Kracauer's grandmother, or Barthes' mother) but it is the body made of an industrially produced representation (the female star) and its technical reproduction. As Kracauer would be the first to point out, it is precisely in the investment of desire into the figure whose body is made up of invisible printed Benday Dots that the libidinal splitting occurs, at the level of the image as much as at the level of the psychic formation, investing the photographic medium with the condition of fetishism in an almost ontological fashion. Kracauer thereby anticipated a whole set of painterly concerns which would re-emerge in the work of Roy Lichtenstein and Andy Warhol in the early 1960s, shortly before Richter was to join them in the pursuit of understanding how the registers of fetishistic desire and of sign exchange value had gradually displaced presence, corporeality and the mnemonic experience and how these changes would inevitably alter the face of painting as well. Yet neither Kracauer's theoretical investigation nor Richter's artistic project are motivated by a nostalgic claim to reconstruct a fiction of an authentic identity centered in the body or the aura and the artisanal artefact. This dramatically separates their endeavours from Barthes' *Camera Lucida* which in fact attempts to resituate the bodily memory within the image of the mother and attempts to imbue it with an experience of phenomenological authenticity.

By contrast, it seems that Richter is engaged in a different project altogether: first of all, he attempts to explore the various registers of photography as the representational system within which historical repression is physically enacted and transmitted. The notorious attraction of post-war German artists to the banality of German consumer culture which governs Richter's extensive perusal of the material of the first four years of the *Atlas* collection (another example would be Polke's iconography) could find an additional explanation here: that it is not just a variation on the themes of Pop Art (which it certainly was as well, inasmuch as Pop Art had itself incessantly posed the question of the possibility of authentic experience under the reign of totalized commodity production). More specifically, what becomes evident in Richter's archive of the imagery of consumption is the underside of this peculiar West German variation on the theme of banality: the collective lack of affect, the psychic armor with which Germans of the post war period protected themselves against historical insight.

Banality as a condition of everyday life appears here in its specifically German modality as the condition of the repression of historical memory, as a sort of psychic anaesthesia. Banality as a condition of aesthetic posture, its counterpart, is of course proclaimed by Richter as well, explicitly when he states notoriously that «...the most banal amateur photograph is more beautiful than the most beautiful painting by Cézanne...».

Once again, two attitudes are joined here that make it doubly difficult to recognize the project of the *Atlas*: first of all, in its slightly juvenile assertion of a radical anti-aesthetic position, Richter associates himself publically with an avant-garde posture that had recently been revitalized in Pop Art's rediscovery of Duchamp. From a position quite typical for post-war German artists, primarily oriented toward the New York and Paris activities of the moment rather than toward the overshadowed legacies of the historical German avant-garde of the 1920s, Richter explicitly credits the work of Robert Rauschenberg with having provided his introduction to the collage/montage aesthetics, while claiming that he was either totally unaware of the photomontage practices of the Weimar Dadaists or that he was outright hostile to whatever model of political agitation in photomontage he might have seen in the work of John Heartfield during his life in the German Democratic Republic. This paradoxical historical and geo-political shift poses a number of additional questions in the reading of Richter's photographic archive.

First of all it poses the question of how the principle of random accumulation operates under substantially different historical circumstances, i.e. at a moment when randomness and arbitrary juxtaposition are not only functioning as established aesthetic procedures, but also as socially enforced legitimation of anomie disguised as an advanced state of individual independence. Collage aesthetic in Rauschenberg's hands had re-inaugurated the elimination of authorial choice and artistic authority by intrinsically linking authorship to the actual conditions of experience within advanced consumer culture, where the formation of exchange-value residing in the sign solely determines the constitution of the identity of the consuming subject.

Clearly, in the post-war moment, techniques of decentering the subject and dismantling authorial claims had changed once again in the transmission from Duchamp to John Cage, one of the formative figures for Rauschenberg's collage culture. It is not easy to determine whether, in what was now the period of the neo-avant-garde, the radically subversive decentering of the (bourgeois) subject had just become a principle of affirmative indifference towards subjectivity altogether (e.g. Cage's Zen approach); or whether, in the post-war recurrence of these strategies, the politically enforced elimination of subjectivity necessitated this aesthetic recourse to structural, perceptual and cognitive anomie, since this model alone seemed to enact the decreasing validity of concepts of communicative action, self-determination, and transparent social organization.

Lastly, and most importantly perhaps from the perspective of this essay, such an attitude provokes the question of how and whether this insistence on anomic banality (even if given only as a posture) and the aesthetic project of dismantling the armor of psychic repression could ever be reconciled. This question will be partially answered by Richter himself, since already in the twelfth panel of the *Atlas*, presumably dating from around 1964-1965, a first set of images suddenly emerges from within the overall banality of the found photographs, rupturing the entire field. This puncturing positions the *Atlas* project suddenly within the dialectics of amnesia and memory that we have attempted to explore in this essay. Functioning in the manner of a *punctum* within the previously continuous field of banal images and their peculiar variation on the condition of the *studium*, the first set of photographs of victims from a concentration camp functions now as a sudden revelation: that there is still one link that binds an image to its referent within the apparently empty barrage of photographic imagery and the universal production of sign exchange value: the trauma from which the compulsion to repress originated. Paradoxically, it is at this very moment that the *Atlas* also yields its own secret as an image collection: a perpetual pendulum between the death of reality in the photograph and the reality of death in the mnemonic image.

BETWEEN THE FINE ARTS AND THE MEDIA (THE GERMAN EXAMPLE: GERHARD RICHTER)*

Jean-François Chevrier

Before approaching the work of Gerhard Richter, it is important to clarify the similarities and above all the differences between the uses made of photography in the early sixties by the artists of the Düsseldorf vanguard, on one hand, and by their American counterparts, or immediate predecessors, on the other. Bernd and Hilla Becher's project is reducible neither to the procedures of conceptual art, nor to the formalist stances of pop art derived from the models of the mass media.[1] Richter, on the contrary, owes a great deal to the model of pop art. Born in East Germany in 1932, he emigrated to the West 1961 and was studying at the Düsseldorf Academy at the moment when he discovered pop art, a pictorial possibility radically distinct from what he had known in the East, and from what he first encountered and experimented with after coming to the West. Richter had begun his career as an East German painter in relative conformity to the norms

* Text based on a lecture given in the Walker Art Center (Minneapolis) on the occasion of the exhibition *Photography in Contemporary German Art: 1960 to the Present* (February-May 1992).

of socialist realism; he had however become aware of the abstract alternative offered by the *informel* movement, presented in the fifties as the characteristic trait of democratic art, notably at Documenta II in 1959. It was to this trend that he initially allied himself. In 1962, the date of his first exhibition (with Manfred Kuttner at the «Junge Kunst» gallery in Fulda), he showed a group of works in the *informel* style; none of them survive today, for he destroyed them all when he realized he had taken a wrong turn.[2] Immediately after this exhibition Richter saw the reproduction of a work by Lichtenstein in a magazine. This discovery precipitated his development. He had already begun to use photographs, but Lichtenstein's example showed him that he had to simplify, sticking to the photographic model and renouncing any addition of painterly or symbolic signs exterior to the unified facture of the *tableau.*** Rauschenberg himself «was too artificial, and too interesting. He didn't have this astonishing simplification.»[3] A few months later, Richter and Konrad Lueg Fischer presented themselves at Ileana Sonnabend gallery as «German Pop Artists», and in October of 1963 the two of them—together with Sigmar Polke—organized their famous exhibition-performance, *Leben mit Pop: Demonstration für den kapitalistischen Realismus* (Life with Pop: Demonstration for Capitalist Realism), in the Berges furniture store in Düsseldorf.[4]

When he speaks of this period, Richter sets himself apart from the constructivist, utopian abstractionism of the Zero group, but he strongly emphasizes his debt to Fluxus, with the one reserve that the principle of «dé-collage» (reinterpreted in the German context by Wolf Vostell in 1962, after its invention in Paris by Hains and Villeglé) always remained foreign to him. He also acknowledges the

** [Translator's note: The author uses the word «tableau» to designate the historical form, developed out of easel painting, in which the image is presented as a frontal, autonomous plane; certain contemporary photographers (and the «photopainter» Richter) have re-established this specific form, in contrast to the reproducible, disposable media image].

influence of the dadaist model and particularly of Duchamp, whom he associated with Beuys at that time (Beuys had actually been invited to participate in the *Life with Pop* exhibition).[5] It would be quite mistaken, then, to ascribe Richter's photorealism in the 1960s solely to the model of pop art, forgetting all he owes to the German and European ambience of Fluxus. One can even draw convincing analogies between the grayed and blurred effects of Richter's photographic paintings of 1964-1965 and the exploration of «moved» or «streaked» shots by a photographer like Peter Keetman, who is more easily associated with the Zero group than with the American avant-garde.[6]

Richter's recourse to photography, beginning in 1962 and especially in 1963, immediately presented the visual signs of a double postulate. On one hand, it shared in the dada-inspired desire for a clean break (anti-art), as well as in the need to simplify painting. Like the work of Lichtenstein and Warhol, it opposed both the rhetorical pathos of late Abstract Expressionism and the picturesque effects of assemblage *à la* Rauschenberg. Photography became an instrument of the «anti-sensibility» which Ivan Karp, one of the early champions of American pop art, posed as the defining characteristic of «common image painting» in 1963.[7] On the other hand, Richter's approach did take into account the emotional impact of the photographic image, integrating an iconographic diversity that remains foreign to all formalist systematization, whether abstract or representational. Photography was also a way of introducing existential content —direct, immediate, and also very «common»—into a pictorial rhetoric too exclusively centered on either the subjective resonances of gesture and material, or the idealization of geometric construction. It would seem that Richter's specific understanding of photography had no equivalent in American art beyond Andy Warhol, and even Warhol restricted himself, in the sixties and seventies, to the repertories of the portrait and the sensationalizing media image. Richter in contrast allowed himself an almost encyclopedic field of exploration.

What was so unusual and so profoundly European in Richter's attitude, and specifically in his use of photography in 1963, becomes clear from a consideration of his position ten years later, in 1972. This was the moment when he presented his work in the German pavilion at the Venice Biennale and exhibited for the first time at the Documenta. In the months preceding and following these two exhibitions, he gave the interviews and wrote the letters that still constitute the best description of his overall project. He had to situate himself in an artistic context where his specific intentions were all too likely to dissolve in multiple confusions. His first priority was to set himself apart from photorealism, then triumphant in the United States. At the year's end, the magazine *Art in America* published a special issue in which Robert Bechtle—considered the leader of the movement on the West coast—enumerated the requisite conditions for a proper use of photography: «There's a lot of danger there. The danger of making finished photographs, for one. I have to be careful that they are really lousy photographs that will allow the completion to take place in the painting. If the photograph is too good and can stand as a finished work of art all by itself, there is no reason to make a painting from it. I also feel I must avoid a too candid type of photography: it's very easy for that quality to creep in when using a 35mm camera.»[8] Richter, who risked being taken for a pioneering photorealist, sought at all costs to avoid any such association. Since 1967 he had regularly painted small non-representational works, parallel to his photographic *tableaux*. At the Venice Biennale he presented foliage *tableaux* in a larger format, including the famous triptych *Ohne Titel (Grün)* (Untitled [Green]), which bears the number 318 in the inventory he keeps of his own production. These works are freely derived from photographs, but the exuberance of the painterly gesture pulls them away from the model of descriptive objectivity and the precise rendition of nature; thus they effect a kind of slippage from photopainting into abstraction, but without cutting the latter off from the photographic model.[9] After the Venice Biennale, Richter radicalized this passage to abstraction with the series of huge informal *tableaux* called *Rot-Blau-Gelb* (Red-Blue-Yellow). Questioned for a special dossier in *Chroniques de l'art vivant* on «hyperrealism», he declared that the photorealists «seem to believe in what they are doing. They have found their salvation once and for all; they are capable of doing photorealism until the end of their days. For my part, I am quite unable to believe so strongly. There is no possible salvation.»[10]

In the course of this same interview he also defined, better than he has done anywhere else, the reasoning behind his use of photography (and not just the kind of practical conditions stressed by Robert Bechtle). He distinguished two reasons. One is traditional, the one Matisse once gave to explain his recourse to photography as a tool for portraiture. «Photography», Richter said, «keeps you from stylizing, from seeing "falsely", from giving an overly personal interpretation to the subject.»[11] The other explanation, which he actually offered first, is rather more original: «A photo is already a little *tableau*, although it is not yet completely that. This character is irritating and pushes you to want to transform it definitively into a painting.» The painting, in short, fulfills the photographic *tableau*. But this fulfillment has nothing to do with Bechtle's «completion». Indeed, Richter had already declared in the course of a preceding interview, published in the catalogue of the Venice Biennale: «I do not wish to imitate a photograph; I want to *make* one.» To this he added: «I am making photos with different means and not pictures which resemble a photograph.»[12]

These two statements have been frequently quoted since their publication, but their significance in the context of photorealism and the aftermath of pop has been somewhat neglected, along with their resonances in Richter's own oeuvre. The interview in *Chroniques de l'art vivant* illuminates both these matters. Where the photorealists monumentalize a descriptive image and avoid «a too candid kind of photography» (preferring the clean finish of a more commercial, professional image), Richter seeks on the contrary to seize an excess of description. He is far more attracted by «banal» snapshots than «artistic, composed» photographs; the latter are «deeply impoverished images, with their play of light and shadow, their harmonies and compositional effects. By comparison, the family photo, with everyone plunked smack in the middle of the image, is literally overflowing with life.» This *overflow* is what interests him, and this is exactly what one sees in his abstract *tableaux* from 1972 on, beginning with the series *Ohne Titel (Grün)*. There lie the similarities and differences with Warhol as well, at least with the Warhol of sensational images, who discovered in the shock effect of press illustrations and the accidents of silk-screen reproduction an echo (albeit parodic) of the pathos of Abstract Expressionism.

Richter had first declared, as a provocation, that he found «some amateur photos better than the best Cézanne».[13] In a 1985 interview he affirmed: «I used the so-called banal to show that the banal is the important and the human. The people whose images we see in the newspaper are not banal, they are only banal because they are not famous.»[14] One can hardly imagine a better response to Warhol's celebrated declaration on the media's power to give anyone fifteen minutes of fame. Richter sees no need for painting to meet the challenge of the mass media by appropriating their power; he does not compete with the media by transforming himself into a public figure. Where Warhol precipitated the transformation of the bohemian artist into the cultural entrepreneur, Richter maintained that the historical presentness of painting is to be found elsewhere than in preprogrammed avant-garde effects. The Duchampian principle of indifference was a model for both artists, but one took it as an end in itself, while the other used it as a means to pull free from a constrictively defined range of options, thus assuring the continuing mobility of pictorial activity.[15] Finally, Richter upheld the divide between public and private. He sought to draw the general from the particular—and refused to limit the general to the particular—while Warhol denied these distinctions. For Richter, therefore, the imagery of family albums was not reducible to its apparent banality, because painting could fulfill the use-value of this imagery, as a generality no longer limited to a specific emotional involvement. Things were quite different for Warhol: a painting conceived in terms of exchange value could only produce an effect of presentness by the irregularities (the accidents) of its reproduction. Warhol was only able to use family photos on a single occasion, in 1963 when he decided to make a historical portrait of Rauschenberg, a more-or-less ironic act of identification directed toward the man who was in the process of becoming the new hero of American painting after Pollock. He entitled his composition and all its variants *Let Us Now Praise Famous Men*, in reference to the cult book by James Agee and Walker Evans.[16]

For Warhol, the common was either what everyone knows (celebrities) or simply the indifferent, fulfilled in death. His work is obsessed with death as necrophilic spectacle, its impact annulled by repetition and by the affective indifference which ensues, much as our subjectivities are equalized by media conditioning. Many critics have remarked that Richter's photographic paintings also develop an insistent iconography of death.[17] But this iconography is constantly contradicted, not only by an imagery of natural beauty (which can also be brought back to the principle of indifference) but above all by a vitalistic (and realistic) conception of pictorial activity. Like Warhol and the majority of post-expressionist artists since Jasper Johns, Richter considers painting primarily as a way of seeing. To create a painting is to fulfill something seen in the secondary reality of the painted image. The initial reality, the model, is no longer a motif *à la* Cézanne, but a photograph, that is to say, already an image. Here, Richter is closer to Lichtenstein—the early Lichtenstein—than to Warhol: the model image must be fulfilled in its singularity, it must be unified (and magnified) by the pictorial work, and not multiplied by a new process of reproduction. He is not so much interested in the iconic value, nor in the traumatic shock of the thing photographed, but in the latent power of the image itself, which calls for pictorial fulfillment—because this power, in its generality, is already that of painting. The pictorial model that Richter found in photography in 1962-1963 was, therefore, the image «literally overflowing with life», as an alternative to the mannerist exuberance of *informel* art. Ten years later, in 1972, this model would allow him both to reinvent *informel* art and to affirm the continuing significance of romanticism.

A letter addressed to Thomas Ammann in February 1973 sums up these two points perfectly. Richter describes the *jungle pictures* presented at the Venice Biennale: «Pictures that emerge, that grow from the making, not "creative" in the sense of this mendacious word (I mention that because I loathe the word so much)—but certainly creaturely. In order to illustrate the fascination that jungle-like intertwining forms have on me: as a child, after I had eaten all my food and while my supper plate was slightly greasy, I daubed loops with my finger, curves that constantly cut across each other and produced spatial structures that changed according to the light, that could be reshaped endlessly. I find this changing and allowing to flow, relativizing, more attractive than fixed form, than set signs. This all has something to do with the *informel*, which suits me very well, because it is the opposite of death, which anyway does not exist, because it is uninteresting. As I now see it, all my pictures are actually *informel* (the glasses anyway, unfortunately I have not got any further with that)—with the possible exception of the landscapes. A picture by Caspar David Friedrich is not a thing of the past, the only things of the past are some of the circumstances that caused it to come into being, e.g. certain ideologies; over and above this, if it is "good" it affects us, beyond ideologies, as art, which we go to some lengths to defend (perceive, exhibit, make). Thus one can paint like C. D. Friedrich "today."»[18] In the course of the interview with Irmeline Lebeer for *Chroniques de l'art vivant*, Richter had claimed to make «an authentic historical reference to romanticism», which he clarified by stating: «That is what sets me apart from the hyperrealists representing the present world with its automobiles, freeways, etc. For my part, I paint historical paintings.» For him, the present is not limited to the spectacle of contemporaneity; history is also a part of it. And when Lebeer asked him, «Is the romantic period closer to you than our own?», he replied: «No, I simply believe that we have not yet gone beyond romanticism. The paintings of this period still form a part of our sensibility; otherwise we wouldn't look at them anymore. Romanticism is far from having been liquidated. Just like fascism.»

* * *

In the context of a vanguard exigency of modernity, Richter stood back, adopting a posture of historical distancing and integration into nineteenth-century artistic culture. But this position makes no appeal to the eclectic academism that so largely characterizes the «neoconservative postmodernism» of 1980s painting; nor does it demonstrate any satisfaction with a lighthearted derision of modernist precepts.[19] Richter refers to Friedrich and romanticism after contrasting the overflow of the photographic image to the hermetic closure of the Cézannean *tableau*, celebrated by the ideologues of an anti-media art.[20] Thus he indicates that the cultural history in which modern art shares is a process of incomplete remembrance: fragmentary, but at the same time foundational for the present. Modern art is not an inheritance to be squandered in the exuberance of pastiche, but a demand for timeliness, for presentness. This demand was met in an exemplary way by Courbet, who achieved a transfer of the thing seen into the painted image, reworking and surpassing the performances of the photographic imprint.[21] But the exigency of presentness must itself be actualized, without forgetting or repressing the romantic past. In the mass-cultural imagination, the romantic heritage is loosely identified as a «romanticization» of the past, and of a present absorbed by the past. Snapshot recording continually confirms this equivalence, to the extent that it fixes the future image of a present which *will have passed*, transforming the present into a future content of memory. Employed as a mode of historical writing, the future perfect of recording also constantly threatens to reinstate nostalgia and to secure its domination over present experience.[22] By specifying his pictorial use of photography—or rather, his photographic conception of painting—with «an authentic historical reference to romanticism», Richter transforms the romantic kitsch of mass culture. So doing, he recovers a critical presentness for romanticism in an art exposed both to nostalgic reification and to appropriation by the culture industry.

What has not been «liquidated» in romanticism is its program of redeeming modernity, or «modern life». This is what gave the movement a revolutionary accent at the beginning of the nineteenth century, and later constituted the ideological basis of fascism in its dream of a new, organic mass community, exalted by the grandiose spectacle of the cultural war industry. Yet when Richter referred to the example of Friedrich in 1972, he set himself apart both from the dogmatic precepts of late formalism and from the fanaticism of the present («the present world with its automobiles, freeways, etc.») in the work of the photorealists. His romanticism is not a backward-looking reaction, but an articulated, conscious, modern resistance to the industrial model of progress which enforces the assimilation of artistic activity to an aesthetic technology.

This properly pictorial position can be resituated in a much larger context, as the remark to Irmeline Lebeer shows clearly enough. In the years around 1968, in Germany as in the United States and France, a more or less activist neo-Marxism grew out of the critical examination of the cultural—and no longer just economic—conditions of modern alienation; it was characterized by a strongly utopian romanticism of resistance, even of combat. As early as 1918, just after the First World War, Ernst Bloch's *Geist der Utopie* (The Spirit of Utopia) had launched a revival of revolutionary romanticism, denouncing the effects of capitalist modernization as «transcendental uprooting», a loss of *Heimat* (home, hearth). Nor did this spirit of resistance disappear. In Germany, the generation of 1968 was just as marked by Herbert Marcuse as by Andy Warhol. In France, the philosopher Henri Lefebvre, who inspired the Situationist International, had published his *Critique de la vie quotidienne* (Critique of Everyday Life) in 1947. His reference to the model of the rural community wiped out by industrial development is not without analogy to Bloch's position. A decade later, the year of the Situationist International's formation, an article by Lefebvre entitled «Revolutionary Romanticism» stated the following: «All romanticism is founded on discord, on doubling and splitting. In this sense, revolutionary romanticism perpetuates and even deepens the earlier romantic doublings. But these doublings acquire a new meaning. A positive distance can be taken from the present, the real, the existent, a distance that augments possibilities, without any flight into the past.»[23]

Defiant of all ideological programs, Richter could not subscribe to any kind of revolutionary terminology, particularly since the notion of «revolutionary romanticism» had been used by Jdanov in the notorious 1934 speech at the Soviet Writers' Congress, to support the new official doctrine of socialist realism. Nonetheless, Lefebvre's manner of formulating the presentness of romanticism clarifies the historical position where Richter locates his pictorial activity. The very possibility of painting depends, for him, on a transformation of the romantic inheritance, despite its exploitation by fascism. Because the history of this exploitation endures, in the very form that Bloch (in *Erbschaft jener Zeit* [Heritage of this Time]) and Benjamin had begun to analyze in the thirties, the matter becomes all the more urgent. Mediated, in the strict sense of the word, by photography—the first of the mass media—romanticism's presence in Richter's painting consists of the *effective recognition* that nostalgia for an organic, preindustrial community is now indissociable from its mass-media treatment, inaugurated by fascism and pursued today by the culture industry. The problem is therefore one of pictorially reappropriating a «mass-mediated» romanticism. Here lies Richter's contribution—an artistic contribution—to the reactualization of the romantic utopia corrupted by Fascism and Stalinism.

Like every city dweller, Richter perceives nature as a collection of images or *tableaux* which signify the ineluctable loss of the «hearth», the «lack of homeland» (*Heimatlosigkeit*) described by Bloch and Heidegger as a distinctive condition of modern man.[24] The indifference of nature—which Rilke, at the beginning of this century, wished to recognize as «a liberating parable for our destiny»[25]—can more crudely appear as simple stupidity, at least insofar as it is not infused with human feelings. In Richter's *oeuvre*, beginning with the first abstract *tableaux* (the first to be explicitly presented as such) and even more pronouncedly since the mid-1980s, the stolid flatness of the photographic image constantly recalls the unmitigated obviousness of the spectacle of nature, in contrast to the expansive effects of the large abstract *tableaux*. Although it can elicit a nostalgic tone —«a type of yearning for a whole and simple life», as Richter said in 1985—this spectacle of nature always remains detached from the kinaesthetic diversity that mobilizes, in the pictorial gesture, what Merleau-Ponty called «the immemorial background of the visible.» It is as though the full frontal visibility of the photographic *tableau* prohibited—and therefore summoned—the physical assumption of the visible.[26] Indeed, there is no longer any trace here of an «overflow» of life, but the fact of a confrontation that calls for a pictorial response, alone capable of «cracking the spectacle-form» (Merleau-Ponty). «My landscapes», noted Richter in 1986, «are not just beautiful, or seemingly nostalgic, romantic and as classical as lost paradises. They are above all "mendacious", even if I did not always find a way of showing precisely that. And when I say "mendacious", I mean the ecstasy with which we look at nature, but nature that is against us in all its forms, because it knows neither sense nor mercy nor sympathy, because it knows nothing, absolutely nothing, is absolutely without mind or spirit, is the total opposite to ourselves, is absolutely inhuman.»[27] With a kind of growing rage, the note continues: «Any beauty that we see in landscape, any enchanting coloration, peace or violence of mood, gentle lines, magnificent space and goodness knows what else is a projection of ours, something that we can switch off, and then be able to see at the very same moment only the terrifying hideousness and ugliness of it all.» Here the execration of nature matches the intensity of romantic hymns of adoration. One can only reject—and not just condemn—what is beyond the sphere of the law: «Nature is so inhuman that it is not even criminal. It is nature that we must essentially overcome, reject...»

Richter generally speaks of his photographic landscapes in more measured terms; he assigns them a functional role as a springboard for abstraction, and is seemingly satisfied with their sentimental and nostalgic resonances, inherited from historical models as well as from habits of reverie nourished by kitsch.[28] But this function of springboard, through the very force of the contradictions it mobilizes, cannot be exercised without violence. The execration of nature expressed in the 1986 note is a *«rage de l'expression»*, in the phrase of Francis Ponge. It becomes particularly striking, with all its intimate, idiosyncratic dimensions, in the small painted photographs (photos covered over in paint) of 1980.[29] Richter is too suspicious of expressionist compulsions to develop the gesture of overpainting very far (as does

Arnulf Rainer, for instance). Nonetheless, this series links quietly back to the destructive impulse that animated the 1962 work *Tisch* [Table], with which—quite significantly—he later decided to open the chronological inventory of his production.

At a thirty-year distance, this *tableau*—the opening piece in the retrospective at the Tate Gallery in London (October 1991-January 1992)—allows us to understand not only the initial situation of the painter-photographer in the early stages of his career in the West, but also his current situation, after the series *18. Oktober 1977*. Richter himself has provided all the necessary indications. Recalling that the photo he used had been taken from the Italian magazine *Domus*, he stressed that this *tableau*—unlike many others which he painted, then destroyed or overpainted during the period immediately after settling in the West—can mark a point of origin for his work, insofar as the pictorial blurring of the photographic motif resolved the problem of giving body to the image.[30] He goes on to evoke the earlier photopaintings. Their content was apparently much more serious, heavy («not taken from magazines like *Domus*»). «There is», he noted, «an illustration of an early one, *Firing Squad*, in one of my catalogues, which contains a partially obscured SS man.» He adds: «It is the sort of image that I used later on when I contrasted pornographic photographs with images from the concentration camps.»

Reintegrated in this narrative sequence, *Tisch* takes on the value of an emblem, or better, a symbolic matrix. When Richter selected this canvas as the origin of his pictorial history, what he sought was to mark off a dividing line from a personal prehistory: «I wanted to make a new start after my work in East Germany, but also after the many pictures I had painted in the West, among which were a number of photopaintings. I wanted to draw a line, indicating that these paintings were in the past.» But one also observes that this prehistory was laden with such violent contents that its rejection necessarily had the effect of a repression, however good its reasons may have been, particularly the rejection of a sulfurous imagery sustained by fashionable Warholian pop art. The association of concentration camp images with pornographic voyeurism was evidently not enough to lift the repression. With their picturesque aestheticization of a sensationalizing imagery, these photos could only confirm the impossibility of mourning the fascist disaster in a German culture aligned on amnesia-prone American capitalism. Thus they remained bound within the *Atlas*. But what is effectively reinstated, or reproduced, through the play of a pictorial covering-over of the photographic image, is the structure of the screen, of the screen memory: painting as the screen of and against a repressed epoch of the past. *Tisch* brought this structure to light. The large abstract paintings spring from it. The small overpainted photographs testify to the rage of expression that this structure could not help provoking, as soon as the painter constrained himself within a private imagery and a romantic iconography of nature. The series of *18. Oktober 1977* can be considered the first possible return to the figurative contents repressed by the institution of a pictorial history founded on the privative structure of the *tableau* (as emblematized by *Tisch*).

Richter has been reproached for taking an interest in the «suicides» of the Stammheim prison, when he himself gave no support to the revolutionary movement of 1968 (of which the terrorism of the Baader-Meinhof gang was the paroxysm and the desperate last bid). In reality, what Richter represents in his images, from his viewpoint as an established bourgeois painter, is the grandeur of an ideological failure in which he had always refused to participate. For years he had repeated that the great political ideologies of the twentieth century, fascism and communism, whose effects he had been able to directly assess, were «criminal». He had chosen, especially since 1976—after the *Graue Bilder* (Gray Paintings)—to carry out his pictorial activity apart from the militancy of «radical» or avant-garde art. In the eyes of the rebels and the revolutionaries of 1968, he had therefore chosen the bourgeois stance, that is to say, a private, or even privative definition of artistic activity. Since 1976, his position had in effect shifted conspicuously away from what had been the program of a movement like Fluxus, whose anti-individualism he had initially shared.[31] And yet when he was asked in 1988 what made the death of the Stammheim prisoners into «an exceptional misfortune» (his own description of the event), he replied: «In the first place, the public ambitions of these people, their non-private, impersonal, ideological motivation.»[32] Faithful to his habits, he did not advance any precise political considerations, he did not speak of the meaning of the terrorist engagement of the Red Army Faction, nor of the nature of the police repression with its secondary effects of the heightened control of civil society (even though the sequence of the first three images is entitled *Confrontation*). On the contrary, he did insist on those aspects of the RAF's ideological engagement which most clearly contrasted with his own situation as a bourgeois painter: its «public», «non-private», «impersonal» character, that is to say, everything he had purged from his own ambitions in the name of a global refusal of ideology. What he sought to show in *18. Oktober 1977* was therefore nothing other than the romantic grandeur of a failure, which he felt obliged to record according to the logic of «historical» painting, the logic he had claimed as his own in 1972 through the reference to romanticism.

Absurd and criminal though it may be, ideological conviction at least had the merit of setting the pathos of a tragic destiny against the indifference of nature, which Richter finally confronted as an absolutely inhuman judgment. Since *18. Oktober 1977*, the private activity of the painter is situated clearly—explicitly, one is tempted to say—between these two extremes. «Photographs», he states, «are almost nature.»[33] They are also the historical trace—or the «mediated» image—of crimes, near or far away, committed across the spectrum of motivation, from the simple gutter-level act to the political assassination; crimes in which the ambivalence of the unconscious is necessarily implicated, alongside the hesitations of moral conscience.[34] Finally, insofar as photographs illustrate the individual's everyday actions and gestures, they form the specific imaginary terrain of private bourgeois life, whose limits art indicates, even if it does not transgress them. For Richter, it is clearer than ever that the domain of pictorial activity, as sheltered as it may be from dogmatic beliefs, is nonetheless entirely exposed to otherness;[35] still more evident is the vanity of the artist's attempt to protect himself from himself by retreating into his *oeuvre*. The *Atlas* is the form of this impossible closure, the palimpsest of the unconscious, both individual and historical, which underlies and tends to overtake the pictorial work.

* * *

In effect, Richter's *Atlas* includes not only the images which have actually given rise to paintings but all the others as well, which have constituted both a fund of iconographic resources and the foundation of the pictorial experience. One may speak of a palimpsest here, if one imagines the painted *tableaux* and the grids of images superimposed, and associates the result with the effects of blurring and erasure used in the pictorial transposition of the photographs. Several buried images then correspond to each *tableau*. Bound together by a thematic or analogical thread, these images constitute the foundation of the *tableau*, the milieu of its inscription, the subtext that resurfaces from one *tableau* to the next.

This function of the palimpsest is precisely what one finds in Polke's work, in a much more explicit fashion. Here as well, photographic materials, among others, are brought into play, through procedures of double exposure and transparency borrowed from film, after the example of Picabia. The Polke-Picabia relationship is well established, but the connection between Polke's cinematic use of photography and certain pre-existing models can cast new light on the romantic reference in Richter's work.

Both Richter and Polke transformed the immediate example of pop art by reintegrating it into a European tradition of painting. Like the American pop artists, they refused the anti-media ideology of modernism, as affirmed in the long, dogmatic exegesis of cubism and of the Cézannean ideal.[36] So doing, they put themselves in a position to reactualize a heritage that had not been absorbed by the Franco-American canon of modernism, and yet did not entail any compromise with the pseudo-alternative of a Germanic «expressionism». Even as photography opened the way to a new repertoire of modernity, it also allowed them to rethink pictorial activity in its relation to media culture. Since they did not renounce painting, they could not help but rediscover—upstream of Duchamp—the manner in which this relation had appeared to the painters who first took stock of photography's capacity to record and reproduce.

Here again, one must look to the decade of the 1850s, marked by a debate on realism which the disputes over photography's status as an art intensified. At just this time, the idea emerged that painting must be more a mnemography than a description. This was at least partially a response to the challenge of photography. In its extreme descriptive precision, the mechanical image fulfilled the mimetic function assigned to pictorial representation. Replacing manual limitation (and its uncertainties) with flawless reproduction, it exposed «incorrect» elements of style in even the most respected masters of the academic tradition.[37] But photography is not only the exact reproduction of an image (comparable to a reflection in a mirror); it is also the fixing, the recording of this image, which is another thing altogether.[38] This capacity for recording is what makes photography a mnemotechnics, allowing for the constitution of archives, public and private. In the 1850s, it enabled exactitude of reproduction to take a step into the background, and aptness or *justesse* (as distinct from exactness) to come to the fore, along with speed of notation. Delacroix does not yet speak of speed in his journal, for it emerged as a distinguishing trait of the photographic inscription only after the handheld snapshot camera became universal, first in the 1880s and later, massively, in the twentieth century. But Delacroix did remark the difference between an overly exact reproduction and an image well-served by «the very imperfection of the process». In 1859 he noted, in the course of a reflection on realism, «When a photographer takes a shot, you never see more than a part cut from a whole. The edge of the *tableau* is just as interesting as the center; you cannot refrain from supposing an ensemble of which you see but a portion, seemingly chosen at random. The incidental is as capital as the principle; most often, it presents itself first and obscures the view. Greater concession must be made to the infirmities of reproduction in a photographic work than in a work of the imagination. The most gripping photographs are those where the very imperfection of the process toward absolute rendering leaves certain gaps, certain resting places for the eye, which allow it to alight on but a very small number of objects.»[39]

For Polke as for Richter, photography sets the impersonality of reproduction against the idiosyncrasies of style. Again, this attitude is not original, since it figures in a long tradition opposing the literal truth of mechanical description to the abusive authority of the masters. It also shares in pop art's appeal to «anti-sensibility», along with the Duchampian call for indifference. But as already stressed in the case of Richter, indifference could neither be an inviolable principle, nor a strict prescription. It was above all a simplifying procedure directed against the pictorial stew of *art informel* and the picturesque character of assemblage. After the appearance of photorealism, with which Richter's work risked being conflated, the model of photographic reproduction as the antithesis of pictorial style became even more clearly insufficient. Through his reference to romanticism, Richter took energetic steps away from any descriptive norm dictated by the increasingly fanatical cult of the immediate. And it is precisely the refusal of realistic or literal description—as achieved by photographic reproduction—that characterizes the romantic position of Delacroix in 1859 and leads him to formulate an aesthetic of photography founded on «the imperfection of the process», in conformity with a mnemotechnic definition of artistic representation. Delacroix does not refuse photography, or at least he does not simply reject it. In 1859, as at decade's outset (when he was a founding member of the *Société héliographique*), he accepts its challenge. But this challenge is double. On one side, that of reproduction, photography finally amounts to a countermodel, a foil above all. On the other side, that of recording, it is very precisely a mnemotechnics with which the painter must openly vie, and which he must transform, fulfill, even transcend, in a mnemography.

Notes:

1. A comparison between Edward Ruscha and the Bechers was attempted in *Typologies*, an exhibition organized by Marc Freidus for the Newport Harbor Art Museum. In the end, this comparison mainly underscored their differences. The «anti-photographic» intent of Ruscha's books—as he himself defined it—can be related to the emergence of a Californian variant of pop art. Typology does not have the value of an investigative method in Ruscha's work, nor that of a heuristic tool, but is above all a pretext for collection and a form of seriality: the specific information furnished by each image is in effect less important for him than the repetitive nature of the conventional motif and of the form of the image on the page. As he made clear in 1965, with respect to his then most recently published book *Various Small Fires*: «One of the purposes of my book has to do with making a mass-produced object. The final product has a very commercial, professional feel to it... I have eliminated all text from my books—I want absolutely neutral material. My pictures are not that interesting, nor the subject matter. They are simply a collection of "facts"; my book is more like a collection of "ready-mades."» (Excerpt from an interview with Ruscha by John Coplans, *Artforum* [February 1965], reprinted in Lucy Lippard, *Six Years: The dematerialization of the art object* [New York: Praeger, 1973], p. 12.) By contrast, and despite the fact that they are often presented in grid-formats, the Bechers' «series» are not essentially serial: the formal variations in each grid spring first of all from the functional nature of the industrial buildings themselves—which retain traits of singularity—rather than from a structure and an ensemble of decisions fixed by the artists.
2. See Jürgen Harten, «The Romantic Intent of Abstraction», in *Gerhard Richter: Bilder / Paintings 1962-1985*, ed. Jürgen Harten, cat. (Düsseldorf, Berlin, Bern, Wien: DuMont Buchverlag, 1986), p. 5 and note 5, p. 57.
3. Interview with Gerhard Richter by Benjamin Buchloh in *Gerhard Richter: Paintings*, cat. Museum of Contemporary Art, Chicago, and Art Gallery of Ontario, Toronto (London: Thames and Hudson, 1988), p. 17.
4. According to Jürgen Harten (op. cit., note 2 above, p. 15), the term «capitalist realism» had already appeared in discussions between Richter, Lueg, Polke, and Kuttner during preparation for a group exhibition held in May 1963.
5. «In 1963 I saw the Duchamp exhibition in Krefeld. It reminded me of Beuys and from then on I began to have a real interest in Duchamp» (op. cit., note 3 above, ibid.). The Duchamp exhibition to which Richter refers actually took place in 1961, not 1963, at the Haus Lange Museum. Richter could not have been very familiar with Beuys' work in 1961. This confusion underlines the degree to which Richter perceived Duchamp through Beuys.
6. See Peter Keetman, *Fotoform* (Berlin: Nishen, 1988), esp. pp. 21, 23, 25. Also compare *Strachus* (1953), no doubt Keetman's most well-known image, with Richter's *Stadtbilder* (Townscapes) from the years 1968-1969. Richter's photographic *tableaux*, like Keetman's image, evoke views of destroyed cities. Concerning *Stadtbild Paris* (Townscape Paris), Richter recently remarked: «When I look back on the townscapes

now, they do seem to me to recall certain images of the destruction of Dresden during the war.» (*Gerhard Richter*, cat. Tate Gallery [London: 1991], p. 126.) One can add that Keetman produced remarkable images of destroyed streets in Munich after the war.

7. KARP, Ivan C. «Anti-Sensibility Painting», *Artforum* (October 1963), reprinted in *Looking Critically: 21 Years of Artforum Magazine*, ed. Amy Baker Sandback (Ann Arbor: UMI Research Press, 1984), pp. 14-15. In particular, Ivan Karp wrote: «Sensitivity is a bore. Common Image painting is an art of calm, profound observation and humorous wonderment without sensibility. It does not criticize. It only records. The attitude of the Common Image painter is whimsical and slightly ironical. The environment is overwhelming, and thus he observes it. He must maintain the sense of the monumentally bizarre without surrealism or else he will defeat his art, just as Abstract Expressionism was winded by lyricism.»

8. Interview with Robert Bechtle by Brian O'Doherty, in «The Photo-Realists: 12 Interviews», *Art in America* (November-December 1972), partially reprinted in *American Artists on Art (From 1940 to 1980)*, ed. Ellen H. Johnson (New York: Harper and Row, 1982), pp. 151-157.

9. In 1972 the idea of abstract painting had not yet appeared by name in Richter's work. The first *Abstrakte Bilder* appear in 1977. But the relation between painting and photographic reproduction is never effaced. In 1978, Richter took over a hundred photographs of a recent abstract painting, which he collected two years later in a book, *One Hundred Twenty-eight Details from a Picture* (Halifax: The Press of the Nova Scotia College of Art and Design. 1978). In the interviews and letters of 1972 he speaks frequently of abstraction; but he also designates the foliage *tableaux* at the Venice Biennale as «jungle pictures», a term which, however, soon disappears and which even at the time did not figure in the titles.

10. LEBEER, Irmeline, «Gerhard Richter ou la réalité de l'image», *Chroniques de l'art vivant* # 36 (February 1973), pp. 13-16.

11. In 1954, in the preface to *Portraits* (Monte Carlo: Éditions André Sauret), Matisse wrote: «I closely studied the representation of the human face by pure drawing, and in order not to give the stamp of my personal efforts to the results of my work—in the way that a portrait by Raphael is above all a portrait by Raphael—I forced myself, around 1900, to literally copy the face on the basis of photographs, which kept me within the limits of the model's apparent characteristics. Since then I have occasionally returned to this manner of working. Even as I followed the impression produced in me by a face, I tried not to stray from its anatomical construction.» Already in 1933—during one of those periods when he had «returned to this manner of working»—he declared to Tériade (in the review *Minotaure*, vol. I, # 3-4): «Photography has really shaken up the imagination, because people have seen things outside of sentiment. When I wanted to unburden myself of all the influences that keep one from seeing nature in a personal way, I copied photographs. We are encumbered with the sentiments of the artists who have gone before us. Photography can

unburden us of previous imaginations.» These passages are reproduced in Henri Matisse, *Écrits et propos sur l'art*, ed. Dominique Fourcade (Paris: Hermann, 1972), pp. 176-177, 126-127. Matisse's recourse to the impersonal exactitude of photography was therefore a way of escaping acquired habits—or in other words, the more-or-less involuntary mannerism of so-called «personal» expression—in order to rediscover a genuinely personal vision. This type of argument was already developed in the nineteenth century by the critic Francis Wey, who remarked on photography's effectiveness in the representation of anatomical traits (for the studies of living models called «académies»); in this, he recognized «the seeds of a revolution against conventional images [*poncifs*].» Liberated from the formula-types of the academic tradition, artists would be able to freely pursue their «fantasy»; thus, writes Francis Wey, «more liberal, less inflexible than the critic withdrawn into his cult of ideal beauty, heliogravure justifies all schools and emboldens the artist to follow his fancy...» See Jean-François Chevrier, editorial, *Photographies* #6 (December 1984), p. 7.

12. Interview with Gerhard Richter, by Rolf Schön, cat. 36th Venice Biennale, German Pavilion (Essen: Museum Folkwang, 1972), pp. 23-25 (first printed in *Deutsche Zeitung*, Stuttgart, 1972). It was also in the course of this interview that Richter very clearly stated his realist conception—in the sense whereby concrete art is a realism—of the photograph as image-object: an objective image which, in its fulfillment and completion, turns into an object. Rolf Schön asks why photography plays such an important role for him. He replies: «Because the photograph which we all use so frequently, each day, surprised me. All of a sudden, I was able to see it differently, as a picture [*Bild*] which conveyed a different aspect to me, without all those conventional criteria which I formerly attached to art. There was no style, no composition, no judgment. It liberated me from personal experience. There was nothing but a pure picture [*reines Bild*]. Therefore, I wanted to possess it and show it—not to use it as a means for painting but to use painting as a means for the photography.» A little farther along, he clarifies his idea, making a distinction between «object» and «objectivity»: «First of all, only photographs can be objective because they are related to an object without being an object themselves. However, I can see them as an object, as well, and furthermore make them one in painting them, for example. After that they can no longer be and are no longer meant to be objective; and they are not to document anything, either, neither reality nor a mode of viewing. They are reality, perception, thus object, themselves, and therefore can only be documented.»

13. This declaration appeared in the text of the Richter-Polke exhibition, Gallerie h, Hanover, 1966; it was reprinted in the catalogue of the Venice Biennale (op. cit., note 12 above, pp. 27-33). The provocation is slighter, or more tightly argued, if one reads the following sentence: «It is not the question of painting good pictures, at all, because painting is a moral act.» Of course one recalls Duchamp's opposition of photography to painting and his use of photography to break with the cubist inheritance of Cézanne. But there are two differences: Richter speaks of «some amateur photos» and not of photography in general, and he advances a criterion of moral judgment which

is foreign to Duchamp's vocabulary. One must also stress that Richter never considered the «found photo»—whether amateur image or press illustration—as a ready-made; for him, photography was entirely removed from all artistic consideration. As he stated to Roald Nasgaard while the latter was organizing the Chicago-Toronto show of 1988: «I wasn't able simply to declare a photograph a work of art by saying it out loud. That wouldn't have even been a ready-made» (op. cit., note 3 above, p. 47). Finally, he has often recalled that in the sixties he chose the photos he wanted to paint without following any predetermined criteria, but he admits that his choice may have obeyed very precise unconscious interests and he refuses to consider it random or indifferent (as a certain Duchampian norm would have it, more orthodox than Duchamp himself, a norm to which Richter may have felt tempted to subscribe). See the discussion with Benjamin Buchloh (op. cit., above, p. 20). As he had already suggested before (in the catalogue of the Richter exhibition at the Musée national d'art moderne in Paris, 1977), Buchloh uses the notion of a random, indifferent choice to evoke Duchamp and Warhol. Richter is completely against this idea («The motifs were never random...»). He makes his intention clear: «They [the photos chosen] very definitely were concerned with content. Perhaps I denied that earlier, when I maintained that it had nothing to do with content, that for me it was only a matter of painting a photo and demonstrating indifference.» Finally, he explicitly ascribes his choices to personal motives: «I looked for photos that showed my actuality, that related to me. And I selected black-and-white photos, because I noticed that they depicted that more forcefully than color photos, more directly, with less artistry, and therefore more believably. That's also the reason why I preferred those amateur family photos, those banal objects and snapshots.» If we go back now to the year 1966, the year of the exhibition in Hanover and the declaration about Cézanne, we must remember that this is precisely the period when Richter approached or tried to approach the most heavily charged iconography, freighted with taboo historical resonances (Auschwitz) and voyeuristic interest (pornography, sexual crimes). Jürgen Harten (op. cit., note 2 above, p. 21) notes: «In 1966 Richter risked the extreme of critical voyeurism when, together with Lueg, he planned an exhibition in the Düsseldorf gallery Niepel on sex and mass murder as unacknowledged realities of the desire to stare. But the attempt to show pornographic pictures and photos from concentration camps side by side failed.» The *Atlas*, in its updates of 1972, "76, and '89, preserves the traces of this attempt. This, in any case, is the context of critical urgency—as contrary as possible to the principle of indifference, lest we identify Richter with Warhol—in which the appeal to an anti-artistic moral criterion must be placed.

14. DIETRICH, Dorothea, «Gerhard Richter: an Interview», in *The Print Collector's Newsletter*, # 16 (September-October 1985), p. 129.

15. In a letter to Edy de Wilde (February 1975), explaining his insistent use of gray since 1967, Richter very clearly states the necessity for the passage through indifference: «For me gray is the welcome and only possible equivalent for indifference, for the refusal to make a statement, for lack of opinion, for lack of form.» Indifference is

therefore included in a dynamic of pictorial activity. The gray differentiates itself and the destructive motivation becomes invisible. For «gray, like shapelessness, etc., can only notionally be real», and the painter «can only produce a shade of color that means gray but is not gray. The picture is then a mixture of gray as fiction and gray as a visible, proportioned color surface.» «In conclusion: I am fascinated by this kind of reduced painting in general because it attempts scrupulously and with great care to achieve correctness or better commitment, because it strives to attain a quality that tends toward validity and generalization. This seems important to me when faced with mindless productivity that is becoming ever less committed.» In *Gerhard Richter*, cat. Tate Gallery (London: 1991), p. 112.

16. See Nan Rosenthal, «Let Us Now Praise Famous Men: Warhol As Art Director», in *The Work of Andy Warhol*, Dia Art Foundation Discussions in Contemporary Culture, # 3, ed. Gary Garrels (Seattle: Bay Press, 1989), pp. 48-49.

17. See esp. Jürgen Harten (op. cit., note 2 above, p. 21). Buchloh disputes this interpretation (op. cit., note 3 above, p. 20), without obtaining Richter's agreement.

18. This letter to Thomas Ammann, from 2-24-73, is reproduced in *Gerhard Richter* (op. cit., note 15 above, p. 111). [This and subsequent translations of Richter have been slightly modified. - Translator]

19. Cf. Hal Foster, «(Post)Modern Polemics», in *Recodings: Art, Spectacle, Cultural Politics* (Port Townsend [Wash.]: Bay Press, 1985), pp. 121-136. «In art and architecture neoconservative postmodernism is marked by an eclectic historicism, in which old and new modes and styles (used goods, as it were) are retooled and recycled... This return to history must be questioned. What, first of all, is this "history" but a reduction of historical periods of ruling-class styles that are then pastiched? A history of victors; a history, moreover, which denies the historicity of forms and materials—an *a* history, in fact. And what, secondly, does this "return" imply if not a flight from the present? Clearly, this was the thrust of eclectic historicism in 19th century art and architecture (especially British): flight from the modern—in its romantic form, from the industrial present into a preindustrial past; in its neoclassical (academic) form, from lived class conflict to the ideal realm of myth. But then this flight expressed a social protest, however dreamy; now it seems symptomatic of sheer *post-histoire* escapism» (pp. 122-23).

20. The opposition between the Cézannean *tableau* and the media image results above all from a theoretical interpretation of cubism as an affirmation of the plastic autonomy of the pictorial object, disengaged from all illustrative or decorative functions. In their 1912 volume, Gleizes and Metzinger wrote: «The decorative work exists only in its *destination,* it is animate only by virtue of the relationships which establish themselves between it and determinate objects... The *tableau* bears the justification of its existence within itself. It can be moved with impunity from a church into a salon, from a museum into a bedroom... It does not go with this or that ensemble, it goes with the ensemble of all things, with the universe: it is an organism.» (*Du «Cubisme»* [Paris: Éditions Présence, 1980], p. 43.) Nonetheless, one must recall that the idea of

the *tableau-objet* underlay the practice of collage and allowed cubist painters to integrate a great diversity of materials into their works, notably elements from print media. Thus, although one can speak of a hypostasis of the plastic value of the autonomous *tableau* in the history of modernism (a tendency exemplified by Cézanne), this history is not founded on a simple rejection of mechanical imagery, which can always be integrated, as raw material, into the pictorial organism. Rather, it is founded on an ideological refusal to assimilate mechanical production—or reproduction—to organic creation. Inherited from the distinction between «liberal arts» and «mechanical arts»—as reformulated in the romantic aesthetics of genius—this refusal was widely expressed among the circles of «modern» artists, particularly with respect to photography. Cézanne was presented as the epitome of the anti-photographic artist, who succeeds in radically detaching the painted image from the relation of literal transcription that photography establishes, with the utmost precision, between the visual object and its reproduction (faithful, exact). This detachment forms the hermetic autonomy of the Cézannean *tableau*, which the Cubist painters (as theorists began to repeat in the 1920s) made into a rigorous principle. In his texts on art from this period, poet and critic Pierre Reverdy gives particular emphasis to the static (and hieratic) value of the perfectly autonomous, hermetic *tableau*. In 1933, he summed up this idea in «Note eternelle du présent» (Eternal Note of the Present), where he describes «the moving secret that resides in a static work whose full force, firmly contained, bursts forth within its own limits!» (*Ecrits sur l'art (1923-1960)* [Paris: Flammarion, 1973], p. 20). In several passages from texts written in the twenties, D. H. Lawrence describes Cézanne's still lifes as the antithesis of the Kodak snapshot, which fixes abstract, disembodied identities. See especially «Art and Morality», in *Study of Thomas Hardy and Other Essays: Works of D. H. Lawrence* vol. 8 (Cambridge University Press, 1985), pp. 163-168. Finally, it may be noted that in a text from the twenties, artist and critic André Lhote denounced the academic productions of the *Salon des artistes français* as «photo-painting», against which, he believed, a conventionalized Cézannism presented an insufficient alternative. See «L'enseignement de Cézanne», reprinted in the anthology of André Lhote's work, *Les invariants plastiques*, ed. Jean Cassou (Paris: Hermann, 1967), p. 40.

21. Richter holds Courbet in particular esteem (indeed, he owns an original canvas). Among the major painters of the nineteenth century, the man recognized as the first modern realist is not only one of the many artists who used photography (see Aaron Scharf, *Art and Photography*, [New York: Penguin, 1974], pp. 131-136); more importantly, he is the figure around whom the debates over the influence and the legitimacy of photography in contemporary artistic practice crystallized in the 1850s. In the eyes of his friend Francis Wey (see note 11 above), Courbet proved that photography could not only furnish painters with useful models, but also with a criterion of truth. It was by following this criterion, and not by refusing it in the name of an historical ideal, that the painter could—and should—surpass the exactitude of photographic reproduction.

22. Here we encounter the ambiguity of romanticism. Like the chronicle, photographic recording can participate in the writing of present history, to the extent that it shows the present as it will be understood later («this will have been»). So doing, photography situates itself between historical action (an always more-or-less blind involvement in the present) and the retrospective interpretation of that action. But at the same time it can also constitute an anticipated nostalgia, a manner of projecting a nostalgic interpretation onto the present and thus transforming it systematically into the past. This ambiguity is characteristic of romantic modernity, whose mode of «presence» consists in the work of memory. One finds traces of it in Delacroix, who notes for example in his *Journal* (April 28, 1854): «As I reflected on the freshness of memories, on the enchanted color they acquire in a faraway past, I admired the involuntary work of the soul, which, in its remembrance of agreeable moments, pushes aside and eliminates all that diminished their charm at the time one actually passed through them. I compared this type of idealization, for it is one, to the effect of beautiful works of the imagination. The great artist concentrates the interest by eliminating useless or stupid or repellent details; his powerful hand arranges and establishes, adds or eliminates, exercising control over objects which are its own. It moves within its domain and invites you there for celebration.» This principle of idealization, itself attuned to the selective work of memory, is linked to the «theory of sacrifices» which, according to Francis Wey, should allow the artist-photographer to avoid or correct the indifferent literality of reproduction. For Francis Wey, photography (heliogravure on paper), in contrast to daguerreotype on metal plates, «is very supple, above all in the reproduction of nature; at times it proceeds by masses, disdaining detail like a skillful master, justifying the theory of sacrifices, here giving the advantage to form, there to the opposition of tones.» See «De l'influence de l'héliographie sur les beaux-arts», in *La Lumière*, # 9 (February 1851), quoted above, note 11. Francis Wey's remarks anticipate the «pictorialism» of the late nineteenth century. A century later, coming after Duchamp and Warhol, Richter obviously does not seek to restore romantic idealism; his photopaintings cannot be considered a neopictorialism. But it is also very difficult to reduce his intention to a transformation of the ready-made (or to a «romanticization» of pop art). Already in a 1977 essay (op. cit. above), Buchloh remarked that the paradoxical application of painting to the ready-made can be interpreted as a reaction to the reification of the idea of ready-made (Duchamp himself was concerned over this, especially after seeing the production of the Nouveau Réalistes). The strategic interest of the paradox of a pictorial ready-made, as timely as it may be, is nonetheless incapable of exhausting everything that is at stake in what Richter termed «an authentic historical reference to romanticism.» To be sure, one cannot argue with the conclusion Stefan Germer draws from the alterations of photographic definition in the photopaintings: «We are consequently confronted with pictures that, awkwardly enough, can only be described in negative terms: they are neither photographs nor paintings, although possessing some of the characteristics of both» (see «Retrospective Ahead», in *Gerhard Richter*, op. cit., note 11 above, p. 26). Still, it seems highly improb-

able that the realist transformation of the photographic image (into the reality of the painted thing) is reducible to the product—or the combined remainders—of a double negation. This transformation mobilizes historical models, both photographic and pictorial, which are themselves transformed, much more than it deploys the «strategy» described by Germer.

23. After its initial publication in the *Nouvelle Revue Française* in 1957, «Le Romantisme révolutionnaire» was reprinted in Henri Lefebvre, *Au-delà du structuralisme* (Paris: Anthropos, 1971). Quoted by Michael Löwy and Robert Sayre, in *Révolte et mélancholie. Le romantisme á contre-courant de la modernité* (Paris: Payot, 1992), p. 228. Löwy and Sayre sum up the development and the historical avatars of «romantic anti-capitalism» (a notion originally advanced by Lukács). An outline of this work was published in English as «Figures of Romantic Anti-Capitalism», in *New German Critique*, # 32, (Spring-Summer, 1984).

24. It is significant that Richter's interest in landscape grows more pronounced after the 1968 *Stadtbilder* (Townscapes), which, in accordance with a now-conventional association of the modern sublime, were immediately followed by views of mountains. Images of the ocean and of vast, deserted expanses correlate with the reference to romanticism (and more particularly to Friedrich). Studies of the sky above Vesuvius, from 1976, can be considered as quotations of the nineteenth-century atmospheric sublime. Finally, in the 1980s, beginning with numbers 549 and 550 of the chronological register—and in counterpoint to the abstract works, increasingly dominant in the painter's production—there appeared a more descriptive, rural, and sometimes even pastoral landscape, of measured effects, nostalgic and rather more picturesque than sublime, clearly partaking of a nature imagery which compensates for urban alienation. This iconographic evolution manifests the accentuation of the theme of *Heimatlosigkeit.*

25. RILKE, Rainer Marie, «Von der Landschaft,» in *Sämtliche Werke* (Insel Verlag, 1965), vol. V, p. 520.

26. It is, in effect, a physical implication in perception as well as in pictorial activity—an implication irreducible to simple visual capture—that allows one to speak of an assumption of the visible. The frontality of the *tableau* accounts for only one dimension of the visible. In *L'Oeil et l'Esprit* (1960), Merleau-Ponty speaks of the «frontal properties of the visible», which are reduced to a «form-spectacle» if they are not associated with an enlivened background movement, enlivening the painter's response: «In the immemorial depths of the visible something moved, caught fire, and engulfed his body; and everything he paints is a response to this incitement...» This dynamic springs from and essentially concerns the movement (even if only ocular) of the seeing body, which itself is part of the visible: «vision happens among, or is caught in, things—there where something visible undertakes to see.» *L'Oeil et l'Esprit* was initially published in *Art de France,* # 1 (1961), pp. 187-208. The English version is «Eye and Mind», in *The Essential Writings of Merleau-Ponty*, trans. C. Dallery, ed. A.L. Fisher (New York: Harper, Brace, and World, 1969); the quotes are from pp. 256 and 283.

27. Note from the artist's journal, 2-18-86, reproduced in the catalogue of the exhibition at the Tate Gallery in 1991, p. 117.
28. See, for example, the remark made to Dorothea Dietrich (op. cit., note 14 above, p. 128) apropos of the landscapes and still lifes he paints «in between the abstract works»: «They constitute about one-tenth of my production. On the one hand they are useful, because I like to work from nature—although I do use a photograph—because I think that any detail from nature has a logic I would like to see in abstraction as well. On the other hand, painting from nature or painting still lifes is a kind of diversion, creates a balance. If I were to express it somewhat informally, I would say that the landscapes are a type of yearning, a yearning for a whole and simple life. A little nostalgic.» In the course of the same interview, Richter makes it clear that he ceased using photography as a model for the abstract paintings in 1980, after *Faust* (number 460 in the register of Richter's works). Abstraction and photography are henceforth quite clearly separate.
29. These little *tableaux*, where paint covers the photographic image instead of reproducing it, constitute the interface between the register of the painted work and the *Atlas*.
30. «The photo for *Table* came, I think, from an Italian design magazine called *Domus*. I painted it, but was dissatisfied with the result and pasted parts of it over with newspaper. One can still see by the imprint where the newspaper was stuck to the freshly painted canvas. I was dissatisfied because there was too much paint on the canvas and became less happy with it, so I overpainted it. Then suddenly it acquired a quality which appealed to me and I thought it should be left that way, without knowing why.» This and the following quotes in the text from the catalogue of the Tate Gallery exhibition, p. 125.
31. See especially the declaration made in common by Richter and Polke (Hanover 1966, note 13 above): «I want to be as everyone is and to think what everyone does and to do what will be done in any case.» This stance in favor of banality and anonymity is clearly Warholian in its formulation. Such a position also owed a great deal to the program of Fluxus, as defined by George Maciunas: «Fluxus is against art as a medium and vehicle for the artist's ego. The task of the practiced art is the solution of the objective problem, they don't have to deal with the artist's personality or ego. Thus Fluxus tends to the idea of the collective, to anonymity and anti-individualism...» From a letter to Tomas Schmit, quoted by Benjamin Buchloh in «Polke und das grosse Triviale», in *Sigmar Polke*, cat. (Tübingen, Düsseldorf, Eindhoven; 1976).
32. Interview with Jan Thorn-Prikker, in *Gerhard Richter. 18. Oktober 1977*, cat. Institute of Contemporary Arts (London: 1989), p. 58.
33. Ibid., p. 53.
34. In 1966, Richter painted the portrait of *Helga Matura* (a prostitute whose murder sparked a flurry of media attention) and above all *Acht Lernschwestern* (the victims of mass murderer Richard Speck's attack on a hospital in Chicago).
35. Death and femininity (associated with youth) are the two manifest forms of oth-

erness, combined in the iconography of *18. Oktober 1977.* Indeed, with regard to the essentially feminine composition of the terrorist group as he portrayed it, Richter admitted in the interview with Jan Thorn-Prikker: «I think women played the more important role: they also made a deeper impression on me than the men» (op. cit., note 32 above, p. 54). One might also remark that this double otherness finds its expression and its equivalent in the black and white—or rather the gray—of journalistic photography, which counters the exuberance of the luminous colors that have characterized Richter's abstract *tableaux* since the 1980s. Returning to black and white, photography once again becomes the other of painting. Here, the indifference of gray is charged with a new pathos. In the light of *18. Oktober 1977,* Richter was even led to redefine the *Graue Bilder* of 1972-1976 (which had provoked the explosion of colors in the first *Abstrakte Bilder.*) Questioned by Gregorio Magnani—«Do you see this series (*18. Oktober 1977*) as isolated, a unique parenthesis, or are you actually revising your relation to "content"?»—he replied: «Yes, this does seem a bit outside of my work. But now when I see the gray monochrome paintings I realize that, perhaps, and surely not entirely consciously, that was the only way for me to paint concentration camps. It is impossible to paint the misery of life, except maybe in gray, to cover it» (see *Flash Art,* # 142 [October 1988], p. 97). Finally, one may note that *Betty,* the portrait (seen from behind) of the painter's daughter, detaches itself precisely from a monochrome gray background, with exceptional descriptive acuity and in very bright, lively colors. Painted in 1988, this portrait thus constitutes the exact antithesis of the female portraits of the series *18. Oktober 1977,* both in its formal characteristics and its chronological situation.

36. On this point, see note 20 above.

37. In his *Journal* (May 21, 1853), Delacroix notes the «incorrectness» of engravings by Marc-Antoine (Marcantonio Raimondi, Raphael's engraver) when compared with nude studies photographed by his friend Eugène Durieu. He experiences «a feeling of repulsion and almost of disgust, for the incorrectness, the manner, the paucity of naturalness, despite the quality of the style»; he can no longer even appreciate this style. He adds, «It is above all upon seeing these engravings, which pass for the masterpieces of the Italian school and which have numbed the admiration of painters everywhere, that one senses the aptness of Poussin's phrase: "Raphael is a donkey compared to the ancients.'» See note 11 above, for Matisse's participation in this anti-Raphaelism provoked by photographic exactitude.

38. The distinction between reproduction and recording is often neglected in discussions of photography and its uses. It is nonetheless quite clear in the research carried out by the procedure's inventor, Nicéphore Niépce. He sought to «reproduce» images (or indeed, «points of view according to nature») as exactly as possible, with the greatest fidelity. This was the first problem. But this reproduction had no interest if it was not durable. It was necessary to durably fix these reproduced images (to «record» them, we would say). Here lay the second problem. The distinction begins to blur when one adds that today, reproduction also designates the multiplication of

an image, notably by photo-mechanical processes, and that this multiplication was another of the early inventors' goals, beginning with Niépce. Reproduction/duplication must nonetheless be distinguished from reproduction/multiplication. A daguerreotype could reproduce an image perfectly, but this reproduction could only be multiplied if it had itself been reproduced by an engraving procedure allowing for the manufacture of prints. Multiplication is only possible in photography on the basis of a negative. As for the notion of recording, it does not bring these ideas of duplication and multiplication into play. On the contrary, it introduces the ideas of inscription and of conservation: without excluding reproduction/multiplication—since one can always reproduce what has been recorded—it involves a temporal dimension that is completely absent from reproduction. Since the spread of snapshot cameras in the 1880s, recording has taken its distances from reproduction/duplication, which supposes the pre-existence of a stable, clearly identified image (of which the *tableau* is the paradigm). The appearance of cinema and sound recording have widened the gap. The snapshot picture participates in recording—and even tends to define photographic recording—because it permits the inscription of a fleeting moment and the conservation of its trace, whereas reproduction, as conceived in the nineteenth century when people spoke of «the reproduction of nature», refers to a fixed, isolated spectacle, from which one may always extract details, or fragments. If many amateur images, including those that Richter describes as little *tableaux* («the family photo, with everyone plunked smack in the middle of the image»), do not correspond to the performances of snapshot recording and seem to be caught up in an earlier aesthetic of the composed *tableau*, it is precisely because the models of these photographs have «taken the pose» and conformed to the canonical image of a memorable instant, withdrawn from time. But even this is a way of recognizing the empire of time over reproduction, by projecting the memorable, reproduced image into the future of rememoration, in the form of the «souvenir». The time of recording transforms the present of reproduction into a future perfect: the living *tableau* will later appear as an image, *it will have been.*

39. DELACROIX, Eugène, *Journal* (September 1, 1859). See note 22 above for the idealization of memory and the theory of sacrifices.

GERHARD RICHTER'S «ALBUM OF PHOTOGRAPHS, COLLAGES, AND SKETCHES»*

Armin Zweite

I

«I see countless landscapes, photograph barely 1 in 100,000, and paint barely one in a hundred of those that I photograph. I am therefore seeking something quite specific; from this I conclude that I know what I want.»[1] This entry in Gerhard Richter's diary from 12 October 1986 is revealing in many ways, but it is also perplexing, if one considers the period in which it was written. The sequence of verbs (see, photograph, paint) is hardly noticeable at first, because it suggests a logical process. He records only a few of the many visual impressions, and of these only a fraction go into the paintings. The medium of photography, in which Richter has been engaged in a variety of ways since the sixties, clearly fills the role of a catalyst for the artist. This is confirmed by the assumption in the second sentence, which speaks of searching, concluding, and objectives, though without specifying the intentions of the artistic act. The photographs

* Revised version of the original text published in the exhibition catalogue *Atlas. Gerhard Richter*, Städtische Galerie im Lenbachhaus, Munich, 1989, and Museum Ludwig, Cologne, 1990.

appear to function almost like a filter of a process, one which applies only to a small portion of his later work: since 1976-1977, the so-called abstract paintings have begun to dominate in his *oeuvre* to such a degree that the figurative works seem more like exceptions to the rule. This does not, however, diminish their significance. Richter's strategy, evident in many of his exhibitions, is to confront very large-format abstractions with individual landscapes or still lifes of modest dimensions. The unusual combination is clearly intended to reveal an identical attitude on which the heterogeneity is based.

Thus, there can be no doubt that photography is a significant aspect of his visual work, but the numbers given in the diary entry (of one hundred thousand impressions barely a hundred photographs, and of those barely one painting) suggest the extent to which the connection between painting and photography has become more lax since at least the mid-1970s, and direct relationships are found only sporadically. New photographs supplement an extensive repertoire of motifs, even though it is utilized less frequently for the paintings. Richter's remark also suggests that to the extent that photography became successively less functional with respect to painting, it was increasingly a means of self-reflection, of memory, or of structural analysis. It would be difficult to explain otherwise why Richter always returns to the camera, particularly when traveling, without following up with a painting of what he has seen. Since he began to use his own photographs as preparatory models for his paintings, this kind of instrumentalization was always there, but never exclusively so, with the result that the medium of photography could exist now and again as an independent genre. The fact that his forty-eight portraits of famous men (1972) also exists as a photographic work (*Catalogue Raisonné* 324a) confirms this attitude, as do the photographic books *One Hundred Twenty-eight Details from a Picture*[2] and *Eis*.[3]

But let us return once again to the opening quotation. What is most surprising, surely, is the conclusion that the painter bases on observation of his own behavior. One cannot help but ask how countless impressions, selective photography, and the rare paintings that are based on photographs are supposed to justify conclusions about the intentions of an artistic work, if that which remains, or is newly created, after this double selection process is in the painter's own words merely «something specific.» The relation between the sensory, the intellectual, and the intuitive is thus open to debate, and at the same time it opens up the question of the legitimacy of painting today. Still, as before we are left without a precise answer, and, as we will see, there are good reasons for this. The beholder is left to examine photographs and paintings that can perhaps help to explain the motivation behind this double distillation process from sensory impressions to the photograph and from the photograph to the painting, and to give some idea what its aim might be.

All this already suggests in outline that Richter is circumventing the semiotic turn of events in modernism that can be defined as the retreat from the object of the representation to the very possibility of representation. Modernism moves from the semantic to the semiotic, from the realized function of the sign to the autonomy of the sign. Though Richter retains the pictorial methods of modernism, he poses the question of the subject in a new way. Thus, he characterizes his own work as a «principled avoidance of the subject», but at the same time has expressed the hope of «getting a subject handed to me on a plate, as it were: one not invented by me, and for that reason more universal, better, less perishable, more generally valid.»[4] It is neither exclusively a case of inventing reality, nor is his effort aimed unconditionally at the imitation of reality, at the reproduction of the actual in realistic paintings. As improbable as it sounds, Richter seems to want to do both things at the same time. In doing so, he reclaims a universal validity for the manifestation of subjectivity, while that which the painter does not invent but «merely» reproduces is meant to be unmistakable and imperishable. The semantic—that is, the signified—is supposed to be subject to the semiotic—that is, the signifier. But the reverse is also supposed to be the case, a paradoxical configuration that results in the abrupt changes in his complex oeuvre that have become a constant source of irritation.

The few statements by Richter on which these claims have been based show that two traditions intersect in his way of thinking. On the one hand, he holds to high modernism's claim that forms of expression are by nature binding. On the other hand, he sees that these forms of expression are individually conditioned and can only develop solely and entirely from the individual's subjective horizon of expectations, and that, consequently, they lend themselves to an irrevocable relativism. There seems to be no resolution to this contradiction, and a synthesis seems inconceivable, so all that remains is to deal with the aporia and to cause it to be seen and experienced in an exaggerated form. As an abstract painter, Richter does not want to be obliged to make the artistic means of his paintings absolute and to depict the means themselves, as it were. As difficult as it may be, he holds to the transcendental claim of the early nonobjective painters to conceive the anticipatory elements of his works conceptually. As a realistic painter, however, he would like to avoid precisely that «profession of faith in the subject» which alone could extricate his works from the sphere of the arbitrary and noncommittal. Richter's is a modern, self-critical consciousness that is revealed in his verbal expressions as well as in his works. Directness alternates with profound desperation; euphoria in creative work changes suddenly into such lasting disillusionment that occasionally all traces of self-confidence seem to evaporate.

In Richter's work, the contradictions of modernism seem to be driven to extremes in one way and brought into a dialectical relationship in various, mutually exclusive modes of representation. Consequently, he has been repeatedly subjected to the thoughtless criticism that he is reacting to the demands of the market simply because his works are divided into sharply defined groups that are entirely unconnected. There is no justification for such criticism, as the visible ruptures result inexorably from the work. His work takes up a problematic that is only rarely addressed in painting, and it seeks an answer in polarization. The unquestionable authenticity of Richter's work essentially precludes the possibility of using historical parallels to undermine the unique role of his work within the contemporary context. One comment, however, may serve to illustrate the observation that the roots of the irrevocable aporias in his *oeuvre* are to be found in the classical avant-garde. At the same time, however, it also becomes evident that Richter deliberately makes the suggested contradiction more distinct and pointed, so that not only the subcutaneous connection with the past but also the radical break with it emerge clearly. One is compelled to go back this far precisely because the process in which nonobjective painting developed out of object-based forms of depiction was a gradual one.

In Kandinsky's case, for example, the anarchy of modernism was expressed not least in the fact that people tore from the «reserves of matter» various forms of embodiment could be divided between two poles, «great abstraction» and «great realism.»[5] Kandinsky characterized great realism, which in his eyes was most purely embodied in the work of Henri Rousseau, as an effort «to exclude from the picture the externally artistic [element] and to embody the content of the work of art by means of the simple ("inartistic") rendering of the simple, hard object. The outer shell of the object, conceived in this manner and fixed within the picture, and the simultaneous exclusion of accustomed, importune beauty reveal in the surest way the inner sound of the thing. By reducing the 'artistic' element to a minimum, the soul of the object sounds forth most strongly from within this outer shell, because external, palatable beauty can no longer distract us.» In Kandinsky's view, abstraction, in contrast to realism, tends «to exclude completely the objective (real) element and to embody the content of the work of art in "non-material" forms.» In abstraction, the inner harmony of the painting is intensified by striking out the real. In abstract paintings, too, it must become possible «to hear the whole world just as it is, without objective interpretation.» This circumscribes precisely, if you will, the contrast between the semantic and the semiotic dimensions of art.

For Kandinsky, the contrast between Rousseau «le Douanier» [customs officer] and his own improvisations and compositions was proof of the polarization of modernism, embodied in works that could hardly be more antithetical. Leaving aside for a moment all the necessary qualifications, one could nonetheless ask whether—and if so, to what extent—Richter's «principled avoidance of the subject» can be associated with the «reduction of the "artistic" to a minimum» that Kandinsky attributes to Rousseau, and whether Richter, in his realistic paintings, is not perhaps also interested in comprehending the essence of the object, that which Kandinsky calls «soul». Richter would surely not use such terminology, which in Kandinsky's case combines metaphorical and synaesthetic elements. Richter's sober manner of expression, however, seems to have a similar aim, when we equate what Richter did not have to invent with what Rousseau «inartistically» reproduces. If we ignore the symbolic tradition that is the basis for Kandinsky's reflections, and if we reduce all the differences between abstraction and realism to the phenomenological aspect, then there is one point in which Kandinsky's and Richter's positions are in agreement, namely, that for both the «great difference on the outside» becomes «a great equivalence on the inside.» Richter seems to pick up on something that fell apart historically—playing out in the works of very different painters—to develop it once again, though under different conditions, in two opposed complexes in his own work. For Richter, of course, what Kandinsky calls the aim of both tendencies—that is, the revelation of the inner harmony of an object (great realism) or of a painting (great abstraction)—has no relevance anymore.

Where Kandinsky still assumed that an identical spiritual principle was revealed in the polarity of artistic forms of expression, and an unswerving truth is manifested in the works, Richter conceives the world as merely an idea and pure projection. In his eyes, nature embodies the absolutely Other, the inaccessible, and the inhuman.[6] We begin to see decisive differences. Kandinsky harbors the firm conviction that art is an instrument of knowledge and that the work is the point where spiritual powers crystallize, but Richter never shared this idealism. Painting is for him neither a means to appropriate reality nor knowledge of the world. In his opinion, it expresses at most an agnosticism, and the works reflect nothing. As surrogates of reality, they remain finally incomprehensible, absolutely lacking in spirit, and full of horror. A pessimism deriving from Schopenhauer colors many of Richter's statements. They reveal the fundamental contradiction that is the basis of his painting. The artistic act should, on the one hand, reflect its obligation to the spirit of utopia, insofar as Richter believes painting to be «intrinsically capable of giving visible form to our best, most human, most humane qualities.»[7] On the other hand, in his view, painting can only create analogies to the ineffable and the nonvisual; it must be «incomprehensible»[8] in order to suggest something that rejects human knowledge on principle. Desperation is the motivation of artistic work, not, as for Kandinsky, emphasis. Richter paints in opposition to better insight, so to speak, because it no longer seems to him possible to comprehend things or situations in painting.[9] Thus, for him, painting is nothing but his «attempt to explore what painting is still able and permitted to do. It was also the sheer obstinacy of carrying on painting, even though nothing seemed to come of it.»[10] Only through negation does art express the ineffable, that is, utopia. This is essentially the standpoint of Adorno, who writes in his *Ästhetische Theorie:* «Through the irreconcilable renunciation of the semblance of reconciliation, art holds fast to the promise of reconciliation in the midst of the unreconciled: This is the true consciousness of an age in which the real possibility of utopia... converges with the possibility of total catastrophe.»[11]

We see, then, how, on the one hand, Richter remains bound to the transcendental claim of painting, but is, on the other hand, aware that this claim can no longer be fulfilled, except as a fiction. Given this understanding, the paintings, no matter whether they are abstract or objective, are merely enigmas or puzzles. «They contain», in Adorno's words, «the potential for the solution; the solution is not objectively given. Every artwork is a picture puzzle, a puzzle to be solved, but this puzzle is constituted in such a fashion that it remains a vexation, the preestablished routing of its observer.»[12] Art as «the highest form of hope»[13] obtains its impulse, in Richter's view, above all from the effort to make this state of affairs, which cannot really be understood, commensurable. It is neither possible to say what he meant to convey in his works nor to rationalize the constant change in method that characterizes his work,[14] and yet painting must be understood as a constant attempt to «picture for oneself what is.»[15] The spiritual content does not hover somewhere beyond the facture, «does not hover above the work's facture; rather, artworks transcend their factuality through their facture, through the consistency of their elaboration.»[16] No matter what the paintings depict, no matter the formal principles on which they are based, they «appear.»[17] But Richter would guard against speaking of the sensory appearance of an Idea in Hegel's sense, because it is precisely that which appears that cannot be named. Richter's art wants to be taken entirely as itself, and it does not permit any view onto the truth about states of affairs that merely appear in appearance and thus sublate it. Art is, in Richter's eyes, appearance in its autonomy, and thus art cannot characterize appearance as appearance. In this view, which hypostatizes aesthetic experience and refers to the act of reflection that paintings bring about, Richter is perhaps following Kant, who freed himself from the determination of a substantial conception of the work of art and believed aesthetic experience existed in the tension between being affected by the senses and creative realization. In a movement that aims at registering what has happened but is nevertheless unending, the act of reflection produces the kind of distracted action that can never be certain, because it always refers to the senses under the sway of the object or the painting.[18] It is the incomprehensible, unaided autonomy of aesthetic phenomena that invites the idea that something can be mastered, and yet it leaves us entirely in the lurch. There seems to be something that wants to be and is able to be understood, but in the end it does not withstand any attempt to grab on to it. This is not merely a matter of deceived expectations, in which it becomes clear that the thing whose existence we conjectured cannot be found anywhere; rather, it simply proves to be of different kind than what the expectation of understanding had assumed.[19] In his work, Richter reflects directly on the impossibility of comprehending the work of art or of bringing the aesthetic experience to an end. Both aspects are reflected in the heteronomy of style and subject matter. Not only does his painting embody these irresolvable contradictions, it is also a constant process.

«Painting is engaged in acquiring, working out, adumbrating a future for itself. It's a future that has yet to arrive anywhere else: but in the picture it's celebrated in advance, as it were.» After everything we have seen thus far, this seems sufficiently decisive and optimistic. But Richter then immediately adds a significant qualification, which amounts to a retraction of his assertion or wish: «If that were to work, yes, that would be good.»[20]

In this domain filled with discrepancies and fissures, the painter is like the mythological figure of Tantalus, but with the significant difference that now it isn't even possible to name the goal toward which his efforts are applied. The attitude expressed in such statements is one determined by historical experience that is ultimately without illusions, an attitude that takes on the traditional challenges but, in view of art's lack of role in contemporary society, can only by meet these challenges in a voluntaristic act. In this act, which is stated in a paradox, appearance is asserted in its autonomy. It goes without saying that the insistence that artistic means follow their own laws does not provide a way out of this dilemma. As early as 1966, he noted: «Making is not an artistic act»,[21] and in 1988 he remarked to similar effect that art is concerned with *what* is to become visible; *how* that it is then produced has nothing to do with art or artistic abilities.[22] Such an assertion might lead us to suspect that the intentional object can be comprehended directly in the act of artistic representation, but other statements by Richter lead us to conclude exactly the reverse, namely, that the incomprehensibility of the artwork is the phenomenon that cannot be comprehended and determined. We are presented with categorical contradictions, in which central importance is assigned to aspects of the work's content, but at the same time these very aspects are denied, and in which, on the other hand, form is characterized as an inadequate means even as it seems to become absolute in the work itself. In view of these contradictions, and against the background of such aporias that play the semantic against the semiotic and vice versa, the question of the function of photography in the artist's oeuvre is raised in a new way.

II

Gerhard Richter first attracted attention in the sixties with paintings based on photographs. Around 1964, he began to save the materials that he used, and in 1969 he decided to combine on panels all the photographs that had either played an important role in his work or could possibly have done so. He arranged the photographs, grouped them in sets that could be viewed easily as a whole, and glued them to standardized mounts of 50 x 65 cm, 50 x 70 cm, and 70 x 35 cm. This body of work, which by then had grown to include 315 elements, was first exhibited in December 1972 under the title *Atlas der Fotos und Skizzen* (Album of the photographs and sketches) in a museum in Utrecht.[23] In 1973, an exhibition in the Kunstverein Bremerhaven followed;[24] in April and May 1974, the Galerie Friedrich in Munich exhibited the *Atlas*;[25] and this was followed by a presentation in the Museum Haus Lange in Krefeld in February and March 1976.[26] When in the midseventies his focus shifted to abstract works, Richter's interest in the *Atlas* withdrew into the background for a time, but the collection has continued to grow, and it now includes more than six hundred panels. The artist continues to add to this work, which lies somewhere between an autonomous work of art and a matter-of-fact documentation, even though for some time now it no longer belongs to him.

The *Atlas* in its entirety, as it exists today, is dominated by photographs. It contains approximately over five thousand individual enlargements, reproductions, and illustrations clipped from other sources. The first panels contain personal photographs evidently taken from family albums as well as reproductions clipped from newspapers and magazines, some of which include fragments of text. The selection concentrates at first on black-and-white images, but by the late sixties Richter shows a preference for color photographs. The formats vary at first, but soon they become standardized in order to permit symmetrical groups of 4, 6, 9, 12, 16, 20, etc., individual photographs. Thus, we are not dealing with an arbitrary accumulation; rather, the *Atlas* is distinguished by a strict structure.

In its thematic arrangement, the landscapes, including both city views and alpine images, are separated from the figurative shots. Isolated objects clearly form yet another category. In addition to photographs and collages of his own and those of others, it also includes diagrams, sketches, and plans for installations. The catalogue from 1972 also illustrates a number of Richter's freehand drawings, though these have since been excluded as not belonging to the collection.

It is unnecessary to describe the *Atlas* panel by panel, nor could we demonstrate all the numerous relationships of Richter's painted works to the corresponding photographic models. For that reason, I limit myself in the following to a few remarks about the major groups [until 1990, in wich the first version of this text was written. *Translator's note*]. References to the paintings are taken from the catalogue raisonné (CR) prepared by Dietmar Elger.[27]

Panels 1 to 15: Figures

Amateur shots of a personal nature alternate with landscape photographs and depictions of consumer goods like automobiles, refrigerators, motor boats, and everyday objects (chairs, telephones, shelves, etc.). Pages from calendars with picturesque regions can be found as well as illustrations from mass media (magazines such as *Stern, Bunte Illustrierte,* etc.) with a particular focus on categories such as fashion, nature, travel, health, and crime. The combination of the heterogeneous material is based partly on criteria of content. The combinations of disparate elements frequently result from formal considerations, for in arranging the images Richter sought to create fields with orthogonal edges in order to subordinate the diversity of the individual bits of information to a homogenous pictorial effect.

Panels 14 and 15 combine material that apparently could not be included anywhere else but that could not be excluded either: furniture (chandeliers, doors), jewelry, art, and sports (the high diver).

Richter used many of the roughly 280 motifs on panels 1 to 15 as models for paintings.

Panels 16 to 20: Concentration Camps

In contrast to Warhol, Richter showed little interest in the perpetrators of the crimes, focusing instead on the victims. There are no paintings based on these disturbing photographs. That these dreadful attestations are rephotographed in shots that are deliberately out of focus (panel 19) and reproduced with distorting colorings (panel 20) suggests that Richter attempted to transform them into artworks, but quickly abandoned the idea. He evidently realized that the horror and terrible suffering that the original photographs reveal could not be subjected to aesthetic manipulations aimed at depersonalization and finally banalization, without jeopardizing the moral stance that Richter had always claimed for art. In the cycle *18. Oktober 1977,* completed in 1988, Richter artistically reflects upon repressed crimes and forgotten sufferings in a way that seems to connect back to these works, though under completely different circumstances (see panels 470 to 479).

Panels 21 to 23: Pornography

Several paintings can be related to this material, though both here and in the other thematic areas it must be emphasized that only a small portion of the shots in the *Atlas* served as models for paintings, and conversely the corresponding source material for several paintings is missing from this compendium. Although in general Richter takes over the photographic models more or less directly, it is striking that the paintings taken from this set of themes are combined images. For example, Richter's *Spanische Akte* (Spanish nudes) and *Pi-Mädchen* (Pi girls) of 1967 (CR 150, 151) are based on more than one reproduction (three for the former, two for the latter).

The photographs from concentration camps did not allow themselves to be transformed into images of the degradation and reification of human beings. In these reproductions from porno magazines, by contrast, this was still possible because these traders in sexuality offer their bodies as commodities. This one-dimensionality apparently proved to be unproblematic in transferring it to another medium, but still it is worth noting that the few paintings based on such subjects play only a marginal role in the artist's oeuvre. Richter does not generally practice social criticism in his painting, though there seem to be hints of it in this complex of works, albeit the manipulations and multiple exposures (panel 23) signal a tendency to veil the motifs or even make them completely unrecognizable. In 1970, the artist responded to such questions as follows: «Like everyone else, I am constantly critical—of countless kinds of things—but not when I am painting.»[28]

Panels 24 to 29: Portraits

Volker Bradke, blurry photographs of studio with a prototype of *Vier Glasscheiben* (Four Glass Panels) from 1967 (CR 160), Mao (model for Richter's collotype of 1968), two friends.

Panels 30 to 37: Famous Men

In groups of thirty to thirty-six photographs, the heads of 270 writers, philosophers, musicians, artists, politicians, and scientists are collected on eight panels. This selection of important men taken from an encyclopedia served as the starting point for the *48 Porträts* (48 Portraits) of 1971-1972 (CR 324/1-48), first exhibited publicly at the Venice Biennale in 1972. Photocopies with lexicographic data on the forty-eight portraits also found their way into the *Atlas* (panel 38). With regard to the artist's criteria for selection, a diagram (panel 39) makes it clear that considerations of content played only a secondary role. What mattered to Richter was above all a superficial aspect: the position of the heads. In the entire ensemble there are only a few pure *en face* views (Kafka), while all the other men turn either to the right or the left. The most extreme examples are three-quarter profile. Thus, we are presented with a scale of slightly modified head positions in which the sitter's gaze is usually at the viewer. The installation sketches also reveal a rigid formalism that forms the basis of the conception. Richter does not, however, view an axi-symmetrical arrangement with Kafka at the center, like the one chosen in Venice, as obligatory. He had other possibilities in mind, even an arbitrary arrangement in a square room. The diagrams reveal

Richter's determination to relate the given architectonic circumstances to the inner structure of his series of portraits. The effort to make an abstract principle absolute, as manifested in the *48 Porträts,* also explains why no women were included. Their different features and clothing would have made integration impossible.[29]

As could be seen in Venice, Richter was less interested in the individual portraits than in the ensemble effect. Using floor plans and sketches of the German pavilion, he developed a precise system for hanging the portraits, which was still included in the publication of the *Atlas* made for the exhibition in Utrecht. Later, it was replaced by the corresponding photographs of the installation (panel 41). As a whole, *48 Porträts* and the associated reflections on form demonstrate Richter's attempt to confront classical principles of ordering, like those he also explored in collaboration with Palermo (*Zwei Skulpturen zu einem Raum von Palermo* [Two sculptures for a room by Palermo], CR 297/1-2).

Panels 42 to 57: Personal Photographs

The twenty-seven photographs of Heinz Kühn, minister president of North Rhine-Westphalia (panels 44 and 45), served as preparation for the two portraits (CR 257/1-2); in the case of Brigid Polk (panels 46 and 47), whom Richter portrayed repeatedly (CR 307-9), a few blurry Polaroids were adequate to paint the full figure of this star from Andy Warhol's Factory; for Barbara Nüsse sleeping (panel 57, cf. CR 281), though, the cropping of the photograph was too close, so Richter felt compelled to fill out the photograph by drawing to create a coherent composition. The various uses to which he put the medium of photography are particularly clear in these examples of portraits.

Panels 58 to 88: Experiments

Double exposures, superimposition of several negatives, graphical reworkings of photographs, alongside clippings from fashion magazines (panel 67), images from the Richter exhibition *Gegenverkehr* (Oncoming traffic) in Aachen in 1969, reproductions of warships, the Vatican Museum (panels 71 to 76), stars, balls, small fires (panels 79 to 84). The material on these panels cannot be reduced to a common denominator. It is worth noting especially the technical manipulations, the results of which Richter repeated in his paintings only rarely. The portraits of Gilbert & George (CR 379-84) should be seen in this context. Many of the sequences had an explicitly personal character and did not serve as preparatory material. In several cases, the exploration of the technical possibilities of photography became an end in itself, and occasionally the series are reminiscent of conceptual artworks. *Various Small Fires* by Ed Ruscha comes immediately to mind when looking at panels 82 through 84. The photographs on panels 64 and 65 are models for the graphic works *Funken* (Sparks) and (Hanover's) *Bahnhof* (Train station).

Panels 89 to 105: Abstraction

This complex of works is dominated by details and enlargements of brush strokes, most of which are arranged in blocks. Sometimes the spatial surroundings of the corresponding painting are suggested (panel 95, cf. CR 273, CR 274; panel 96, cf. CR 271, CR 275). The addition of a human figure gives an idea of the size relationships (panel 103). On several of the panels Richter's systematic procedure can be followed easily. Photographs of creamy streaks of paint in red, yellow, and blue are arranged in rows (panel 100) in order to determine the most interesting structural formations. Mixtures of the primary colors are included in a particular sequence and removed from the other photographs (panel 101). In one case (panel 105), the photographs selected as models for paintings are found on the mounting boards used in the work with gradations in tone as a sequence of the coloristic coordination. Corresponding black-and-white enlargements (panel 104) reveal how Richter accentuated the highs and lows by schematically reworking the reproductions and how he considered subdividing the painting into six vertical bands. The *Atlas* only rarely permits precise insights into the procedure such as these (panels 98 to 105) that led to the three large paintings of 1973 (CR 345/1-3). These large paintings, each of which measures 300 x 600 cm, were commissioned for the headquarters of BMW in Munich.

Panels 106 to 124: Cities

The panels contain approximately one hundred aerial photographs of cities. To these are added photographs of models for cities or housing developments and several collages that record ideas for installations. The corresponding paintings were made primarily in 1968 and 1969, and they vary greatly with respect to both artistic solution and size. The spectrum ranges from small formats (53 x 43 cm) to versions that fill a wall (*Stadtbild Madrid* [Cityscape of Madrid], 277 x 292 cm). If the accent in Richter's objective oeuvre up to this point has been on individual subjects, which despite all the slurring of contours and inner form have nonetheless appeared clearly in the paintings, here he is working from models that suggested another procedure, not least because of the abundance of details. It is an expressive style combines the conglomerate of architecture and streets seen from bird's eye view into a plane formed of gray color values. In doing so, the details are considerably less perceptible; indeed, they seem to be canceled out entirely and subjected to an abstract structure. On the other hand, the vividness of the overall situation is still retained in the painting so that one still has the immediate association of «cityscape» when standing in front of one of these works. Still, everything is highly defamiliarized, especially since Richter tries to exclude significant monuments of the cities from his compositions. For example, in the cityscape of Paris (CR 175), the corresponding model (panel 119) reveals that Richter selected just a detail and cropped out the unmistakable Place Charles de Gaulle with the Arc de Triomphe at its center. The installation sketch on panel 123 permits us a similar observation: the aerial photograph placed in the collage has been rotated 180 degrees, creating an irritation that makes it significantly more difficult to read the photograph. A comparison of paintings that were completed somewhat later (CR 249-51) with their corresponding models (panel 121) shows how rotation, reduction, or enlargement of the detail have dissolved the relationship between the image and its model. It goes without saying that the artist's goal was not simply to make his sources unrecognizable. Rather, he seems to resist taking over the entire motif directly. The «principled avoidance of the subject», the strategy of arbitrariness, takes another form with this set of themes than with the figurative paintings. In particular, the paintings of 1970 that were based on city centers photographed from higher altitudes are reminiscent of the rubble wastelands of bombed cites, an analogy that Richter has confirmed in an interview.[30]

Panels 125 to 130: Mountains

The features that emerged in the cityscapes come to the fore even more succinctly in the paintings related to these panels in the *Atlas*. If the first is simply an enlargement and simplification (CR 181) of the corresponding model (panel 126),what is striking about the large alpine panorama is the release of a broad brush script that sums up the details of the preliminary material (panel 130)—a view of Zugspitze over the Ziller Valley and the Stubai Alps—in broad gestures. As with the cities or housing developments seen from above, in Richter's view, it was the latently chaotic element of «mute stuff» in natural or manmade formations that inspired him to give to his depictions a more universal kind of content.[31] The contrasts of light and shadow, of jagged peaks and broad basins, of steep slopes and deep valleys, of vegetation, snow, and rock are subjected to a dictate of form that at times not only captures the contradictions on a plane but also levels them off (CR 213) so that such works suggest preliminary stages of the painted versions (CR 325 ff.). If in the realistic figurative paintings, for all the arbitrariness of the subject matter, the subjective component of the selection could apparently not be excluded entirely, the mode of representation could at least help avoid anything individual. In the cities and landscapes, this dialectic is reversed in that the motifs seem more universal, more impersonal, and more arbitrary, whereas the style of representation now seems to be borne by a subjective impulse.

Panels 131 and 132: Hitler

These panels with reproductions that Richter made in 1969 but which have left no trace in his painted *oeuvre*, apart from CR 3, were added in the final stage of preparations for exhibiting the *Atlas* in 1989.

Panels 134 to 181: Landscapes

This group, another one that combines various complexes of motifs, is dominated by structural comparisons that are made with the aid of photographs systematically arranged. A number of the illustrations under this rubric can be connected to painted versions. The models for CR 283/1, 284, and 287 are all found on a single panel of the *Atlas* (panel 136). The panels often call to mind a conceptual work, as when branches, clusters of foliage, underbrush, edges of forests, clearings, and so on, are collected in parallel series of images (panels 157 and 158). The monumental *Parkstück* (Park Painting) of 1971 (CR 311), measuring 250 x 626 cm, is based on a colorful collage (panel 155) whose mounting board is filled with traces of work. This is an examplary demonstration of how Richter, without changing the structure of his model, not only displaces the accent by separating out a narrow sequence on the right side that is marked by the two trees standing alone, but also manages an optimal division of the large surfaces of the painting into individual elements. The black-and-white enlargement makes that plausible. Finally, a second photograph of the left section forms the preliminary stage for CR 310, though the man with the cow is left out of the painting.

Frequently, the photographs reproduce particular moods: fog (panels 153-54), moonlight (panel 156), sunsets (panels 164 to 166). Matter-of-fact photographs of New York, for example, or the site of the National Socialist convention in Nuremberg (panels 148 and 151), alternate with kitschy views. The integration of various postcards (panels 175 to 178) indicates that this effect is deliberate. This is also a theme in the paintings. Photographs of a rainbow (panel 169) lead to a corresponding sequence of paintings (CR 261/1-3); individual groups of trees, as unassuming as they might seem (panel 174), can become the starting point for a painting (CR 258), though the *Atlas* also elaborates on the relationship of the painting to the furniture and the spatial ambiance. Summarizing the observations that can be generalized, one comes to the conclusion that there are many overlapping layers in the *Atlas.* The compendium is only partially a collection of models for the paintings; it is too a large extent an instrument of reflections on form that always stand in some relation to Richter's visual work.

Panels 182 to 218: Cloud and Sea Paintings

Without exception, each photograph here reproduces a view of the open sea beneath a cloud-filled sky. What is remarkable is that most are collages, where the edge of the cut is along the horizon: the sea and the sky conform neither in lighting nor in atmospheric mood, and this can be clearly felt even in the corresponding paintings (CR 233 ff.). The irritation is increased in several instances by the appearance of moving water in the upper half of the painting. In at least one case (panel 194), this kind of manipulation serves as the basis for the conception and execution of paintings (CR 244, 245). After a few panels with clear skies and surf are juxtaposed (panels 199 to 202), the panels are dominated by cloud photographs arranged in a strict grid (panels 205 and 206). Here, too, the close connections to the painted oeuvre cannot be missed. The four-part painting *Wolken (Fenster)* (Clouds [Window]) of 1970 (CR 266) goes back to a color photograph that has been reworked and masked (to adjust proportions). In the model (panel 213) for CR 267, one can see how Richter tried out the mixing of paints used for the painting in tiny test patches on the original photo. The large, spectacular cumulus clouds (CR 270/1-3) also have corresponding models in the *Atlas* (panel 212). Panel 218 points to CR 268 and CR 276.

These few remarks ought to suffice here to make it clear that the cityscapes and Alps, seascapes and cloud paintings stand in an inherent relation to one another. This is perhaps easier to see in the photographs and collages of the *Atlas* than in a comparison of the paintings themselves. Whereas the photographs of the first two theme complexes suggested a more spontaneous style of brushwork that could simultaneously augment and resolve the immanent fissures and contrasts, the latter two groups of works privileged a more expulsive style of painting could that transform the clouds especially—which by nature lack concise form—into colorful mists and lighter or darker-shaded veils. In the works of this phase, a painterly bravura is developing that no longer feels a need to secure for itself an objective world, but neither does it want to become an object itself. The juxtaposition of such varied characteristics could easily be misunderstood as eclecticism. Richter himself seemed to confirm such an assessment when in 1970 he stated: «I pursue no objectives, no system, no tendency. I have no programme, no style, no direction. I have no time for specialized concerns, working themes, or variations that lead to mastery. I steer clear of definitions. I don't know what I want...»[32] The polarizations in Richter's oeuvre, which became particularly marked around 1970, point not to this lack of stance that Richter claims for himself in this statement, which is intended as an affront, but rather to an intense search to legitimize his artistic practice. It would be wrong to speak of a cynical attitude; rather, one feels indirectly the knowledge that all styles, all methods, all subjects have long become obsolete. The pseudo-revolutionary pathos of earlier avant-gardes must seem particularly dubious to Richter, as well as to many other enlightened artists, in light of the social contradictions that became impossible to ignore in 1968 and thereafter. Art had no obligatory goal that lay outside of itself, but neither could it connect up to any valid tradition. Relativism seemed insurmountable because it had become so absolute. In this period, when everything seemed simultaneously possible and accessible, one way out, as formalistic as it might seem at first glance, seemed to lie in systematizing the disparate and accentuating mere appearances. The contradictory element needed to be summarized in order to reveal a dialectic unfolding on many levels that could not be grasped from an isolated painting in a museum, a private collection, or an exhibition. The *Atlas* is, at least for the period in which it was conceived, the definitive foundation from which large parts of the painted oeuvre arose. The material that is assembled on these panels is the basis for operations that ties together that which the paintings can no longer unify. The following panels, which move into the center of the compendium, as it were, demonstrate that such thoughts of synthesis could be combined with an undercurrent of harmonic equilibrium.

Panels 219 to 252: Rooms

Earlier panels have already made it apparent that Richter was repeatedly exploring in his sketches the spatial effects of his paintings. On the panels collected here, however, we can see a transformation in that the goal now seems to be to conceive the appropriate architectonic ambiance for large-format paintings. Thus, many of the wall-sized representations give the impression of an opening in the room. In other cases, the wall is clearly separated into partitions into which paintings are inserted. The architecture and the paintings are linked to one another (panels 221 ff.). One collage (panel 223), in which an inner room that is merely suggested opens into a classicizing interior, is particularly informative in this context. Here it is evident that Richter's conceptions for rooms are related not only to comparable works by Palermo but also to older traditions. The other sketches reveal this as well, as when the paintings are given rounded terminations and fitted under lunettes (panel 224). Walls, ceilings, and even floors (panel 222) are broken down by means of illusionistic painting, which is reminiscent of the principles of Baroque decoration, except that Richter separates the planes sharply and occasionally emphasizes the architectonic frame (panel 251, panel 242) to such an extent that the paintings no longer seem like surrogates of reality but must be understood as appearances. This is particularly true of a constructivist subdivision of the walls (panel 250) in which details from cloud paintings are positioned in rectangular fields according to decorative principles. Many of the sketches suggest megalomaniacal pretensions. The human forms seem tiny in contrast to the cosmic landscapes (panels 234, 249, 243), which occasionally recalls the hybrid ideas of the revolutionary architects. All of the sketches take up the same subjects: clouds in the sky, sea, and mountains. In only two cases does the motif of brush marks become the basis for the overarching conception (panels 252 and 231). All of the ideas are for permanent installations. In exhibitions, such ideas could only be realized temporarily and even then in a limited fashion, as in panel 245 which shows an idea for installing his 1981 retrospective in the Kunsthalle Düsseldorf.

What emerges from all these sketches seems, on the one hand, to aim at a devaluation of the autonomy of the individual painting, which is no longer meant to be seen for itself, but instead gains a new function as part of an overall spatial conception. On the other hand, the often oversized formats have a suggestive effect that makes it possible to experience the sublime, bringing into play once again the question of painting's claim on the public. These panels can be read as an attempt to dodge the trend to specialization into various branches and instead to achieve a new symbiosis of space and painting in which each will increase the effect of the other.

Panels 253 to 271: Sketches

For one group of paintings, Richter began not with photographs but with sketches in his own hand. The theme here is essentially the relationship of the picture plane to the picture space, of light and shadow, plasticity and linearity, of rhythm and series, sharpness and blurring, and so on. The contrasts are brilliantly developed in the paintings, and various alternatives are played through in superior style. Richter soon abandoned this complex of works, however, as it evidently seemed to sterile to him. He nevertheless included in the *Atlas* a great deal of material for these works, some of which were quite large. Thus *Balken* (Beams) of 1968 (CR 208/2) corresponds to a drawing (panel 258). The same is also true of *Fenster* (Window) (CR 204) and *Fenstergitter* (Window grates) (CR 207), for which the models can also be identified (panels 257 and 256). Architectonic fantasies for public housing (panel 259) and an underground theater (panel 261) alternate with sketches (panels 262 to 264) for the pedestal and placement of the portrait busts of Palermo and Richter (CR 297/1-2) and designs for furniture (panel 260; see also panels 287 and 288). Several diagrams with constellations are also included here (panels 266 and 267) though their relationship to the paintings on this theme (CR 255/2-4 and CR 224/11-15) is not immediately evident.

Panels 272 to 298: Color Fields

In 1966, Richter created a series of works that marks one extreme in his oeuvre: square or rectangular fields are each given a smooth coat of a single homogenous tone. Sketches from 1966 for an exhibition of individual color panels and a series of portraits are also included here (panel 289). One spies a handwritten remark, which can almost be read as the motto for the later «soft» abstractions: «You see no less by taking a blurry look at one area through a loupe.» In addition to the three primary colors and mixtures thereof, one series of paintings also treats the white-gray-black scale. Thus as many as 1024 (CR 350/1-4), and in one extreme case 4096 (CR 359), different tones are united on a single picture plane. Many of these paintings are reminiscent of the sample chips of paint manufacturers, except in Richter's case the distribution of the blue, yellow, and red tones, and all their refractions and shadings, does not proceed systematically but is instead the result of arbitrary decisions that take into account the current taste of the day. In 1973-1974, Richter took up this group of works again (CR 350 ff.), though now the selection and sequence of colors was given over to chance. Every subjective component was excluded, as Richter drew lots to choose each tone in the sequence. The *Atlas* contains studies for both these complexes that pertain to the proportion of the paintings, their spatial arrangement, the progression of the distribution of the fields, and so on. In addition, ideas for an unrealized project for Kunst-am-Bau (panel 290) are included.

Here the individual colors are cleanly separated, but in the so-called *Vermalungen* (Mispaintings) (CR 325/1-120 ff.) they are mixed. These works can be seen as a negation of everything that had occupied Richter up to this point. Nothing is left here, no motif, no color, no structure. And yet the paintings were too painterly to be considered Minimal Art, as a consequence of the movements on the upper surface of the paint that mark them as traces of a brush. Even at the time, they were considered an expression of indifference, meaninglessness, and avoidance of a statement.[33] Ultimately, they were extreme attempts to represent powerlessness and desperation.[34]

Panels 299 to 309: Vegetation

These panels with photographs from Meerbusch and Corsica are obviously concerned with working out structural problems. Reflections in water are captured along with eddies (panel 301), the delicate branches of bushes on the edge of the shore (panels 299, 300, 302, 303), and exotic forms of leaves and flowers seen close up (panels 304 to 309). In several cases, Richter again takes up the effort to create interesting results through the use of double exposures (panel 306). All of them seem to have been without direct consequences for his painting, with the exception of one small flower painting (CR 425/3). As structural nature studies, however, they are essential requirements for the *Vermalungen* and especially for the abstract paintings up to the present day.

Panels 310 to 321: Landscapes

Of the landscape photographs taken in Italy, only a few have served as models for paintings. For example, panel 311 shows a view of Vesuvius that became the starting point for the paintings of the same name (CR 404-10). The selection and arrangement increasingly confers on the multitude of different subjects and moods the status of an independent genre capable of taking the place of painting.

Panels 322 to 331: Sea Paintings and Clouds

Only a few paintings from 1976-1978 correspond to these 153 photographs, and apparently only one painting (CR 411) can be associated directly with a photograph (panel 322).

Panels 332 to 340: Arosa, Davos

These photographs, especially those taken at twilight, with the sun barely penetrating the clouds (panel 333) and the mountainous world immersed in milky light, were the inspiration for several paintings from 1981 (CR 468/1-3, CR 471).

Panels 341 to 359: Greenland

Of the 220 photographs that are collected on these panels, once again only a very few were later used for paintings (CR 476, CR

496/1-2). These photographs from 1972 did, however, form the basis of Richter's *Eis,* a book of photographs published in 1981 by Galleria Pieroni in Rome.

Panels 360 to 362: Venice

Panel 362 tells us something about the process of the genesis of a painting in that Richter has noted several instructions for the work here: «Not this orange-red evening mood as on the model, but hard midday.» Wiped traces of paint and pencil sketches on the mounting board show that the photographs were used for models (cf. CR 586/1). The same is true of the photographs on panel 360 (CR 586/2-3).

Panels 363 to 373: Landscapes

This complex of works collects landscape photographs from wide-ranging sources. The photographs on panels 363 and 364 repeat four motifs from panel 312, this time with traces of paint on the mounting board. The overwhelming majority of these photographs, which are arranged by content and composition, have had (thus far, at least) no response in the painted oeuvre.

Panels 393 to 394: Betty Richter

At least two of these photographs of Richter's daughter (panel 394) formed the basis for paintings (CR 425/4-5).

Panels 395 to 396: Palazzo Regale

The visual arts appear in the *Atlas* in very few places. Reproductions of two Baroque portraits (panels 9 and 10), a Picasso painting (panel 15), and reproductions of the Laocoon group in the Vatican Museum (panel 72) are the only exceptions. So it is that much more remarkable that Richter included in this collection two panels with photographs from the Museo Capodimonte in Naples, where, shortly before his death, Beuys installed his last large environment, *Palazzo Regale.* Richter can be seen on many of the unpretentious amateur photographs, either alone or with his daughter. These photographs can certainly be viewed as an homage to an artist Richter admired.

Panels 397 to 401: Candles and Skull

For the first time, we are dealing with photographs that reproduce a situation that was conceived in advance. With the burning candles and skull, Richter is drawing on a traditional *vanitas* motif. In several cases, these consist of collages, as the candles are cropped and pasted onto enlargements. A whole series of paintings from 1982-1983 was made from these photographs (CR 497-99, CR 510-12, CR 523/1, CR 545, CR 547, etc.). In this complex of works, the relationship between the photograph and the painted transformation is particularly close, which must be a result of the special character of the photographs, which Richter conceived with an eye to his paintings. It is also interesting that one particularly carefully composed photograph (panel 397) apparently did not serve as the model for any painting. Moreover, as the sketches on the border make clear, Richter arranged the comparatively complex structure of a burning candle, a tablecloth, a skull, and a white rectangle in the background in such a way that either the candle alone or the skull would occupy the central point of the composition (CR 546/2, CR 548/1-2). This is clearly one of the rare examples in which the drawing mediates between the photograph and the painting, contributing to a process of clarification that is guided by an artistic intention. In several cases, a realistic, large-format preliminary painting is transformed into an abstraction (CR 568/1).

Panels 403 to 413: Abstract Paintings

Here, too, we can limit ourselves to a few remarks. Panel 403 reproduces a color photograph of CR 433/2, a painting from 1978 measuring 62 x 90 cm. The markings on the mounting board and the sketched figure of a viewer suggest that Richter repeated the painting in a larger format (CR 434, 1978, 200 x 335 cm). In the latter version, the individual forms begin to blur. The artist occasionally referred to such works as «soft» abstractions. Panel 405 combines four details of a small abstraction from 1976 (CR 398/1, 65 x 60 cm) which then became the preliminary material for four paintings from 1977 (CR 417-20), each measuring 225 x 200 cm. Something similar can be observed in the details from CR 398/3 and the compositions that derived from them, CR 422 and CR 424. In this case, too, details from a small-format work are enlarged to such an extent (300 x 200 and 250 x 200 cm, respectively) that the individual elements begin to dissolve and the transitions begin to bleed. It is possible that photographic experiments led to this aesthetic of mimetic blurring, as can be seen from panel 407, where a detail of an abstract painting is photographed increasingly out of focus until the structure dissolves into an optical conglomerate. Panels 408 and 409 are also related to this one. Panel 411 is significant in that Richter has preserved fourteen different states of a painting from 1978 (CR 432/4). This example can be understood equally well as a process of artistic intensification or as a sign of the futility of labor: The question arises whether the final state of the painting really represents the optimal solution, or whether the painting had simply passed through a series of states of completion before Richter ceased work on it.

Panels 414 to 421: Personal Photographs

The *Atlas* is above all an instrument for work, and only rarely does it serve to record personal experiences and memories. The photographs combined here show the sculptor Isa Genzken, Gerhard Richter's second wife. Nevertheless, this section of the whole does not come across like a fragment of a private album. The sober gaze of the photographer as he records the scene, which seems to lend the photographs an objective character, corresponds to the often cool, distanced expression of the person portrayed. It would be inappropriate to interpret the photographs psychologically, especially since we know neither the intentions behind the images included nor the criteria for selecting them. Still, it is striking how Richter, consciously or unconsciously, excludes his private life, blocking this aspect out of the *Atlas* almost entirely. It is tempting to ask whether the «principled avoidance of the subject» also includes the private sphere, or to what extent the private sphere allows no stance other than the one that is the basis for the work.

Panels 422 to 439: Landscapes

Of these 166 photographs, several served as inspiration for the most important landscapes of the eighties, for example, two paintings titled *Scheune* (Barn) from 1983-1984 (CR 549/1, CR 550/1), *Wiesental* (Valley meadow) (CR 572/4) and *Buschdorf* (CR 572/5) from 1985, and two paintings titled *Domecke* (Cathedral corner) (CR 629/1-2) from 1987-1988.

Here again, it is striking that, in the selection and combination of the photographs for the panels, criteria for ordering are based primarily on form. Thus, the line of the horizon often passes through several rows of reproductions; the lighting and mood remain the same on a panel as much as possible; corresponding angles of view and perspectives are sustained. Again and again, the point is to develop sequences. The panels thus acquire their own aesthetic and are very much more than a mere collection of working materials. Richter photographs almost exclusively land that has been cultivated by man, and yet the landscapes very rarely contain people (panel 424). Occasionally, houses can be seen; rural equipment is never on view, nor are industrial products; and even animals turn up only rarely (panel 455). Even so, they are not always idyllic scenes that accentuate the picturesque, but rather regions that suggest that the destruction of agrarian life has not yet taken place here. In the paintings associated with these photographs, this is all exposed as appearance, though in such a subcutaneous way that this kind of romantic irony is superimposed with a blinding illusionism. It only becomes apparent gradually that the paintings have a false bottom; a dimension that, as it happens, is only implicit in the photographs.

Panels 440 to 444: Still Lifes with Apples and Bottles

As in the experiments with candles and a skull (panels 397-401), here, too, Richter arranges the objects into a still life that he then photographs. The arrangement on the mounting boards is based on aesthetic considerations, as arbitrary as the combinations might sometimes seem. With respect to the motif, the photographs point to some smaller-format paintings from 1984 (CR 560/1-3).

Panels 447 to 459: Various Motifs and Landscapes

This group relates to panels 422 to 439 . They need not, therefore, be discussed in detail, except to say that panels 447 and 451 contain the models for two large-format landscapes from 1987 with the title *Chinon* (CR 644 and CR 645) that depict, barely visible on the horizon, the nuclear power plant located there.

Panels 460 to 467: Toronto, New York, Niagara Falls, Sils-Maria

Panels 468 to 469: Overpaintings

These consist of photographs that were almost entirely covered in paint using a monotype process so that their motifs shine through only partially. They are related to all the photographs in the *Atlas* where traces of paint can be seen on the mounting board.

Panels 470 to 479: *18. Oktober 1977*

The ten panels unite one hundred photographs in two groups. The first five panels contain eight photographs in upright format, arranged in two rows of four; on the other panels, there are twelve photographs in oblong format, arranged in four rows of three. This material is related to a cycle of fifteen paintings in various formats, *18. Oktober 1977,* on the deaths of the leading members of the RAF [Rote Armee Fraktion, Red army faction]: Andreas Baader, Gudrun Ensslin and Ulrike Meinhof. This group of works, unique in Richter's *oeuvre*, which amounts to an attempt to revitalize the history painting, shows how the aesthetic form of a memorial work amounts to a strategy of forgetting.[35] In painting, Richter approaches a repressed event and at the same time pushes it into the distance, so that it eludes the attempt to bring it into the present.[36] Especially given the background of the many abstract works that have largely defined the artist's work in recent years, the boldness of taking such a risk is all the more admirable.

The photographs integrated into the *Atlas* were made after the paintings were completed, whereas the precise photographs used for the painted versions were deliberately left out of the *Atlas.* The relationship of the image to its reproduction is thus, in a sense, reversed. Only in the *Atlas* does Richter follow up on the reproductions of concentration camp photographs from his early period (panels 16 to 20), for which there are no equivalents in the paintings.

III

Looking over this enormous collection of material as a whole, it is nearly impossible to determine a coherent structure with respect to content. In response to changing interests and projects, Richter would vary the material he found appropriate to integrate into the *Atlas,* finding new groupings or leaving out certain complexes of works that seemed to him in retrospect to be unimportant. A comparison with the publication from the exhibition in Utrecht in 1972 makes it clear that he not only rejected the installation sketches from his exhibition for the Venice Biennale (1972), but also the photographs and sketches that were related to prints and the plans for sculptural monuments. Freehand drawings were also left out. Neither is a strict chronology to be found; on the contrary, the rearrangement of many complexes is a conscious effort to break down any conceivable ordering scheme. This is done because Richter views the collection not as a sequence of individual sheets, but as a spatial totality that is experienced simultaneously not sequentially. His precise diagrams for the progression of the walls in the exhibition in Krefeld attest to his effort to give spatial form to his own past in the concrete form of his artistic output. The development in a sequence of sheets is meant to be evident at a glance. Ultimately, it is about the simultaneous availability of problems of content and formal complexes that Richter picks up again after substantial intervals.

If, on the other hand, one approaches it from the chronology of the painted works, then the connections become more and more loose. Of the works produced through 1966 (CR 1-144), about half of the subjects can be found in the *Atlas.* For the later paintings, this is true in a much more limited sense, with the exception of the still lifes (candles and skull). In the latter case, Richter leaves nothing to chance. He takes photographs of situations that are arranged according to a preconceived idea for a painting. Whereas the early panels are dominated by figurative motifs, landscape photographs soon come into the forefront, though they are interrupted again and again by experiments in structure and form. Still, it is striking that entire thematic areas are left out. The world of work and the state of society are excluded entirely. Richter takes up historical and political themes only exceptionally (concentration camps, Hitler, *18. Oktober 1977*), which are somewhat at odds with everything else and pierce the otherwise protected sphere of aesthetic appearance like an insurmountable trauma. Art is touched upon in just a few examples (*Palazzo Regale* by Joseph Beuys). Everything private is reduced to a minimum. The photographs of friends (Palermo) and family members (wife and daughter) define two salient positions in the kaleidoscope of images, but they should not be seen primarily as personal disclosures by the artist; the attitude manifested in many of these photographs is too abstract and distanced for that.

If the name *Atlas* (Album) signals an intention to represent, arrange, and make available the entire repertoire of motifs, then this compendium only partially satisfies those expectations. In many cases the panels offer a key to the paintings, especially where the traces of work are clearly evident. Nevertheless, over long stretches the photographs composed in groups and series, the collages, the experiments in form, and the sketches testify an independent course of research that runs parallel to the painted oeuvre. It is not so much the painter who peers through the viewfinder of the camera, but the amateur who is transformed into a conceptual artist only through the prints and enlargements. The *Atlas* comprises highly varied regions that are explored into the smallest detail, but it also touches upon areas in which Richter quickly lost interest, which are, therefore, not explored more deeply.

Although there does not appear to be a binding unity in the content, the heterogeneous elements are subjected to a clear organizational scheme. The solid scaffolding—seen in the blocklike arrangement of reproductions that are generally the same format, the standardization of the mounting boards, and the coherent frame—binds together the disparate content and suggests homogeneity. It is a dialectic of order and latent chaos, of reflection and spontaneity, of universal and individual, of sharpness and blurring, of abstraction and empathy, which develops in a collection of material that is continually overflowing. The *Atlas* gives almost no hint of the personality of the artist, as it is not an intimate diary. Richter is experimenting, documenting, and archiving in such a matter-of-fact way that he himself does not become a subject of that task. Consequently, the *Atlas* is more than the sum of its parts. It can be understood as an autonomous work that combines a manageable amount of diversity with exacting form; it provides fragments of a picture of the world, but it refuses to be taken as a coherent world picture. The *Atlas* is conceived with its exhibition in mind. It is not primarily designed as a biography of works that opens up the iconography of the painted oeuvre, but as an autonomous opus with a well-defined aesthetic that is intended for a public. In the compendium, the obstinacy of the visual sense is systematized, and at the same time the documentation of the aesthetic gaze is divided into facets such that the totality of accumulated information acquires something impenetrable. The *Atlas* is two things at once: a facilitating instrument and an independent object, biographical journey and exercise in content and form—an open work that accompanies and complements the self-contained paintings.

IV

In his beautiful essay *La chambre claire: Note sur la photographie,* Roland Barthes notes that a photograph is always invisible. It is not that which we see.[37] What this means is, first of all, the undeniable fact that in viewing photographs we do not immediately and habitually separate the signifier—that is, the photograph—from the signified —that is, the object reproduced. Starting from a universal observation—that, especially in amateur photographs, we see primarily what is depicted, while in painting we also simultaneously reflect upon the means of representation—Barthes distinguishes between two aspects of photography, for which, for lack of better alternatives, he chooses Latin terms: *studium* and *punctum.* In his definition, the *studium* —Barthes uses the term in the sense of *enthusiasm* or *interest*—triggers a culturally mediated reaction, a universal affect, whereas the second element breaks through this, seizes and irritates the viewer, even giving him or her a prick (*punctum*). *Punctum* is that which goes beyond the universal interest. *Studium,* according to Barthes, is always encoded, but *punctum* is not.[38] *Punctum* is the «beyond», as if the photograph were to awake in us a desire and curiosity to transcend what it permits us to see.[39] *Studium* marks the wide-ranging field of unconcerned desire, various interest, inconsequential taste. At most, it produces a vague, slippery interest in people, events, and things. One is not touched beyond that, either in a positive or negative sense.[40] *Studium* is based on experience and education, and it allows one to make inferences about the photographer and his or her intentions. *Punctum,* by contrast, has an expansive, metonymic quality that can exist in the surprising or disturbing details of the photograph, which fill the whole picture, as it were.[41] Starting from this phenomenology, it seems clear that the photographs in Richter's *Atlas* were selected solely on the basis of *studium.* They are almost exclusively photographs that awake at most a moderate interest; photos that are neither touching nor astounding, neither fascinating nor shocking, with a few exceptions —the photographs from concentration camps, of Hitler, of the members of the RAF and their deaths. The characteristic element is almost always occluded, and the banal and interchangeable are foregrounded, so few of the reproductions in the *Atlas* really capture us. The channeled superabundance, the arrangement into small groups, and the formation of larger series aggrandize the process of leveling-out that is potentially inherent in the overwhelming majority of the works. And yet this blocking of communication leaves one phenomenon untouched that is also expressed pointedly in the *Atlas:* the interblending of reality and the past. What we see in the photographs in the *Atlas,* whether they were taken by Richter himself or are merely found objects, is something that once was, that lies in the past, that no longer exists, at least not in that form. This is particularly true of the photographs of people, but it also applies to the landscapes and still lifes. In both cases, there is no future. In truth, the photograph does not awaken a memory; rather, it blocks memory and becomes its very opposite, its «counter-memory», as Barthes says.[42] The photograph's *noema* lies in its intractability, in the «that-has-been.»[43] The amateur is usually understood to be someone who is either unwilling or unable to achieve mastery of a profession, but in photography the situation is reversed: here, the amateur is the precondition for the professional, because he is closer to the *noema* of photography.[44]

This 1980 essay on photography by Roland Barthes helps to focus on the concept that occupied Richter from the beginning. A text collage published together with Sigmar Polke in 1966 states succinctly: «I consider many amateur photographs better than the best Cézanne.»[45] And in 1970 the painter responded to a question about his criteria for selecting photographs as models for his paintings: «Perhaps the choice is a negative one, in that I was trying to avoid everything that touched on well-known issues—or any issues at all, whether painterly, social or aesthetic. I tried to find nothing too explicit, hence all the banal subjects...»[46] Banality, avoidance of the *punctum,* emphasis on the «counter-memory», that is what Richter sees in the photograph, and he wanted to transfer these principles to painting. In doing so, he wanted to steer clear of everything aesthetic, so as not to set obstacles in his own way.[47] In his eyes, every means was justified to avoid the appearance of art.[48] The genre-specific categories of painting broke down in amateur photographs and magazine illustrations, where the signified was immediately in evidence as something already past. The photograph «had no style, no composition, no judgment. It freed me from personal experience. For the first time, there was nothing to it: it was pure picture.»[49] Under such premises, the photograph is, for

Richter, not a means to painting; rather, painting is a means to photography.[50] As he understands it, his paintings are photography by other means,[51] and for precisely that reason they cannot be assigned to painting in the traditional sense. Painting «as far as its photographic qualities were concerned—was mostly not so good as photography, because it also had to work as painting, which meant a completely different quality.»[52] This other quality that makes painting painting had to be eliminated, and the emphasis had to be placed on precisely that element of painting that is characteristic of the photograph. By favoring the *studium,* Richter places the accent on the *noema,* but by means of the blurring of his paintings, he breaks down the symbiosis of reality and the past that exists in the photographs. As the reality of the content decreases, the element of the past increases in magnitude. The signified comes directly in view and simultaneously withdraws. Blurring is imprecision, and that means difference with respect to the object represented.[53] This counteracts the very thing that makes photography valid. Ultimately, it is naive realism that makes it possible to accept as realistic a reproduction that can seem objective not only with respect to its correspondence with the reality of things themselves, but also with respect to its social function. Namely, when society grants the patent for realism to photography, as it were, all it does is confirm by means of a tautology that the image of the real which is true to photography's objective means of representation is also genuinely objective.[54] Seen in this way, Richter's paintings are useless to society as photographs. The blurring disappoints the expectation of the immediate presence of reality, without, however, invalidating the traditional means of perception. Thus, in the artist's view, his painting as a photograph cannot provide a substitute for reality, but at most a «crutch... to get to reality»,[55] which forces the viewer to stumble into a zone where language is totally absent,[56] because when the social function has been rescinded, the possibility of communication is also cut off.

The emphasis on a lack of art, that leaves everything mute and points to an ephemeral sphere where things and forms become merely fleeting shadows of themselves, is especially characteristic of the first panels of the *Atlas* and the associated photographs. The idiosyncrasies of Gerhard Richter's *oeuvre*, however, are also evident when they are seen in the relevant historical context. Just one example will suffice to illustrate that. In 1966, Richter expressed his reflections on the relationship of photography and painting in a surreal fantasy, the very absurdity of which is revealing. «All painters, everybody», he wrote, «ought to paint from photographs. And they should do it the way I do (including the selection process). Then such paintings should be exhibited everywhere, and everywhere they should be hung—in homes, restaurants, offices, stations and churches, everywhere. Then great painting competitions would be held. The jurors would assess the entries according to theme, rendering and speed, and then they would award medals. Every day, on television and on the radio, there would be reports on the latest paintings. Eventually, laws could be passed so that people could be punished for not painting enough copies of photographs. This would have to go on for 400 years or so, and then painting from photographs should be banned in Germany.»[57] Such a statement is no doubt reminiscent of Andy Warhol, and in the early sixties Pop Art, as Richter repeatedly emphasized, provided an important impetus for his work.[58] Warhol remarked in passing that he had always wanted to paint pictures of the same size. «I think every painting should be the same size and the same color so they're all interchangeable and nobody thinks they have a better painting or a worse painting. And if the one "master painting" is good, they're all good. Besides, even when the subject is different, people always paint the same painting.»[59] The same principle (painting from photographs) had a far more radical consequence in Warhol's work, in that even the results can not longer be distinguished. But this is precisely what Richter wanted to avoid. So, despite the comparable stance, the differences in their painted oeuvres are striking. Whereas Warhol aims at the surrogates of media reality, and he defines the relationship between the painting and its model as a tautology, Richter, by taking the photograph seriously as a photograph, wants something entirely different. One example can illuminate this difference. Richter, too, painted Jacqueline Kennedy (CR 29), but unlike Warhol he does not reproduce in an endlessly repeatable series the clichéd image of the president's wife in mourning. Instead, Richter makes her unrecognizable, because, as he said, he was embarrassed to paint Jacqueline Kennedy. «It was such a beautiful photo, of a woman crying», as he expressed it later.[60] Neither the incessant superficiality and the abandonment of the simulation of reality nor the aesthetic of consumption interested him; rather, it is the *noema* of the photograph of the crying woman, which he presents in a singular, irreproducible painting, at the same time slurring and masking the sitter's distinctive features to turn her into an anonymous figure.

Here, too, a paradoxical double strategy manifests itself, one that posits affirmation and negation in one. The authenticity of past events is isolated from the identity of the person affected by them. The dialectical relationship of photography and painting not only promotes the process of depersonalization, but it also blocks the memory of the specific incident. Seen in this way, it becomes possible to understand again, in its full multiplicity of meaning, Richter's attempt to confront the medium of photography. It also reveals the extent to which epistemological doubts pervade his artistic work.

This was decisive for his stance in the sixties, and it seems to have ended with a series of four paintings, *Tourist mit Löwe(n)* (Tourist with Lion[s]) (CR 368-370/1), based on a film that recorded an accident in a French wild animal park.[61] From the midseventies on, the paintings based on photographs begin to disclose a different attitude, and thus it is not surprising that Richter gradually began to revise his conception. In 1984, he expressed himself in a way that runs counter to what he said around 1970. Looking back, it seemed to him as if he had always been concerned to bring out the message in the photographs and to emphasize their dignity in transporting them into art.[62] In 1988, he said: «The motifs were never random; I had to make much too much of an effort for that, just to be able to find photos I could use.»[63] And when he goes on to say that even in his earlier work he was most definitely concerned with content, and certainly not in demonstrating indifference, one is inclined to say that such a remark might pertain more to the realistic paintings made around that time. The latter frequently seem sentimental, even to the artist, when he introduces personal elements into them.[64]

This is not the place to question the validity of this kind of statement. Instead, let us once more emphasize in conclusion that large parts of the photographic material preserved in the *Atlas* are not merely testimony to indifference, banality, and «counter-memory», for they go far beyond that to sum up a description of loss of epic proportions. More and more, the *Atlas*—having largely abandoned its original intention of keeping his original tasks, materials, and concepts accessible—seems to have become an instrument that holds on to that which was, that which lies in the past, that which cannot be repeated. Although a direct connection to the painted oeuvre is only rarely to be found, perhaps the photographs have for Richter a function that goes beyond that of evidence. The question arises whether they do not perhaps contain, in condensed form, something the abstract paintings are no longer able to transport directly. In the *Atlas,* the world of people, things, and nature appears under the sign of ephemerality. In the abstract paintings, by contrast, everything appears open to the future under the sign of hope. Or at least that is clearly how Richter sees it himself, when he says: «The only paradox is that I always begin with the intention of obtaining a closed picture, with a properly composed motif. Then, with a relatively big effort, I proceed to destroy this intention piece by piece, against my own will almost, until the picture is finished—that is, until it has nothing left besides openness.»[65] The *Atlas* and the painted oeuvre correlate in such a way that the richness and complexity of the former, which neither takes the full measure of the artistic arsenal nor catalogues it fully, give it a significance that has hardly been recognized yet for work as a whole. The polarities intersect: With respect to content, the *Atlas* is closed insofar as it points to a past that is overwhelmingly anonymous, whereas the paintings, in Richter's view, preserve a utopian element in the appearance of future possibilities. With respect to structure, the situation is reversed. The *Atlas* is open insofar as it is constantly changing and able to grow, whereas the individual paintings, once they have left the studio, must be viewed as completed. It is not least this binary dialectic and the internal double strategy—which we were able to demonstrate particularly well with reference to the photographs—that make the *Atlas,* despite its austere visual charms, such a fascinating work.

Notes:

1. RICHTER, Gerhard, *Gerhard Richter: Werken op papier, 1983-1986; Notities, 1982-1986,* exh. cat. (Amsterdam: Museum Overholland Amsterdam, 1987), p. 15. [*Translator's note.* Reprinted in Gerhard Richter, *Text: Schriften und Interviews,* ed. Hans-Ulrich Obrist (Frankfurt am Main: Insel Verlag, 1993), p. 121. Translated by David Britt as *The Daily Practice of Painting: Writings, 1962-1993* (London: Anthony d'Offay Gallery; Cambridge: MIT Press, 1995), p. 130. Cited hereafter as *Text* and *Daily Practice,* respectively].
2. RICHTER, Gerhard, *One Hundred Twenty-eight Details from a Picture,* The Nova Scotia Pamphlets 2 (Halifax: Press of the Nova Scotia College of Art and Design, 1980).
3. RICHTER, Gerhard, *Eis, 1973-1981* (Rome: Edizione Galleria Pieroni, 1981).
4. RICHTER (see note 1), p. 15. [*Text,* p. 121; *Daily Practice,* p. 130].
5. KANDINSKY, Wassily, «Über die Formfrage», in *Der Blaue Reiter,* ed. Wassily Kandinsky and Franz Marc, new documentary edition by Klaus Lankheit (Munich: Piper Verlag, 1965), p. 147 ff. [Translated in Kenneth C. Lindsay and Peter Vergo, eds. *Kandinsky: Complete Writings on Art,* vol. 1, 1901-1921, (London: Faber and Faber, 1982), p. 242 ff.].
6. RICHTER (see note 1), p. 11. [*Text,* p. 115; *Daily Practice,* p. 124].
7. Gerhard Richter, interview by Wolfgang Pehnt, *Künstler im Gespräch,* ed. Werner Krüger and Wolfgang Pehnt (Cologne: Artemedia, 1984), p. 131. [*Text,* p. 110; *Daily Practice,* p. 118].
8. RICHTER, Gerhard, *Abstrakte Bilder, 1976-1981,* exh. cat. (Munich: Jahn, 1981), p. 16. [*Text,* p. 91; *Daily Practice,* p. 99].
9. SAGER, Peter, «Gespräch mit Gerhard Richter», *das kunstwerk* (July 1972), p. 27. [*Text,* p. 64; *Daily Practice,* p. 69].
10. *Künstler im Gespräch* (see note 7), p. 125. [*Text,* p. 106; *Daily Practice,* p. 114].
11. ADORNO, Theodor W., *Ästhetische Theorie* (Frankfurt am Main: Suhrkamp, 1970), p. 56. [Translated by Robert Hullot-Kentor as *Aesthetic Theory,* Theory and History of Literature 88 (Minneapolis: University of Minnesota Press, 1998), p. 33].
12. ADORNO (see note 11), p. 184. [*Aesthetic Theory,* p. 121].
13. «Gerhard Richter», in *documenta 7,* vol. 1, exh. cat. (Kassel: Paul Dierichs, 1982), p. 84 ff. [*Text,* p. 93; *Daily Practice,* p. 100].
14. DIENST, Rolf-Gunter, *Noch Kunst: Neustes aus deutschen Ateliers* (Düsseldorf: Droste, 1970), p. 199. [*Text,* p. 58-59; *Daily Practice,* p. 63-64].

15. HAASE, Amine, *Gespräche mit Künstlern* (Cologne: Wienand, [1981]), p. 113. [*Text,* p. 87; *Daily Practice,* p. 95].
16. ADORNO (see note 11), p. 129.
17. Gerhard Richter, interview by Zdenek Felix, quoted in Ulrich Loock and Denys Zacharopoulos, *Gerhard Richter* (Munich: Verlag Silke Schreiber, 1985), p. 37 n. 53.
18. BUBNER, Rüdiger, «Über einige Bedingungen gegenwärtiger Ästhetik», from 1973; reprinted in *Ästhetische Erfahrung* (Frankfurt: Suhrkamp, 1989), p. 38.
19. BUBNER (see note 18), p. 41.
20. *Künstler im Gespräch* (see note 7), p. 129. [*Text,* p. 107; *Daily Practice,* pp. 114-115].
21. Catalogue from Galerie h, Hanover, 1966; reprinted in «Gerhard Richter», catalog of the thirty-sixth Venice Biennale (Stuttgart: Cantz, 1972), p. 30. [*Text,* p. 43; *Daily Practice,* p. 49].
22. Gerhard Richter, interview by Benjamin H. D. Buchloh, in *Gerhard Richter: Paintings,* ed. Terry Neff, exh. cat. (New York: Thames and Hudson, 1988), p. 18. [*Text,* p. 131; *Daily Practice,* p. 140].
23. RICHTER, Gerhard, *Atlas van de foto's en schetsen,* Hedendaagse Kunst, Utrecht, 1 to 30 December 1972.
24. Helmut Heissenbüttel, «Gerhard Richter», in *Gerhard Richter,* exh. cat. (Bremerhaven: Kunstverein Bremerhaven, 1973).
25. GLOZER, Laszlo, «Die Vor-Bilder der Bilder», *Süddeutsche Zeitung* 97 (24 April 1974): p. 36.
26. *Gerhard Richter: Atlas der Fotos, Collagen und Skizzen,* Museum Haus Lange, Krefeld, 8 February to 14 March 1976.
27. RICHTER, Gerhard, *Bilder, 1962-1985,* ed. Jürgen Harten with a catalogue raisonné by Dietmar Elger (Cologne: DuMont, 1986). [*Translator's note.* See also Kunst-und Ausstellungshalle der Bundesrepublik Deutschland, *Gerhard Richter,* vol. 3, *Catalogue Raisonné, 1962-1993* (Stuttgart: Edition Cantz, 1993)].
28. DIENST (see note 14), p. 195. [*Text,* p. 57; *Daily Practice,* p. 62].
29. VAN BRUGGEN, Coosje, «Gerhard Richter: Painting as a Moral Act», *Artforum* 23, no. 9 (May 1985): p. 91.
30. VAN BRUGGEN (see note 29), p. 86.
31. RICHTER (see note 22), p. 21. [*Text,* p. 136; *Daily Practice,* p. 146].
32. DIENST, Rolf-Gunter, *Deutsche Kunst: Eine neue Generation* (Cologne: M. DuMont Schauberg, 1970), unpaginated. [*Text,* p. 53; *Daily Practice,* p. 58].
33. *Künstler im Gespräch* (see note 7), p. 124. [*Text,* p. 105; *Daily Practice,* p. 112].
34. VAN BRUGGEN (see note 29), p. 88.
35. STORCK, Gerhard, «Ohne Titel (Gemischte Gefühle)», in *Gerhard Richter: 18. Oktober 1977,* exh. cat., Museum Haus Esters Krefeld, Portikus Frankfurt (Cologne: Walther König, 1989), p. 13.
36. GERNER, Stefan, «Ungebetene Erinnerung», in *Gerhard Richter* (see note 35), p. 51.
37. BARTHES, Roland, *La chambre claire: Note sur la photographie* (Paris: Éditions du Seuil, 1980), p. 18. [*Translator's note.* English translation by Richard Howard as

Camera Lucida: Reflections on Photography (New York: Hill & Wang, 1981), p. 6. Cited hereafter as *Camera*].

38. BARTHES (see note 37), pp. 48 ff. [*Camera*, pp. 26-27].
39. BARTHES (see note 37), p. 93. [*Camera*, p. 59].
40. BARTHES (see note 37), p. 49. [*Camera*, p. 28].
41. BARTHES (see note 37), pp. 74, 77. [*Camera*, p. 45].
42. BARTHES (see note 37), p. 142. [*Camera*, p. 91].
43. BARTHES (see note 37), p. 120. [*Camera*, p. 77].
44. BARTHES (see note 37), p. 154. [*Camera*, pp. 98-99].
45. Catalogue of the Gallery h, Hanover, 1966 (see note 21), p. 32. [*Text*, p. 49; *Daily Practice*, p. 55].
46. DIENST (see note 14), p. 194. [*Text*, p. 57; *Daily Practice*, p. 62].
47. DIENST (see note 14), p. 198. [*Text*, p. 58; *Daily Practice*, p. 63].
48. SAGER (see note 9), p. 16. [*Text*, p. 62; *Daily Practice*, p. 66].
49. Gerhard Richter, interview by Rolf Schön, *Deutsche Zeitung*, Stuttgart, 1972; reprinted in «Gerhard Richter» (see note 21), p. 23. [*Text*, v67; *Daily Practice*, p. 73].
50. RICHTER (see note 49), p. 23. [*Text*, p. 67; *Daily Practice*, p. 73].
51. RICHTER (see note 49), p. 23 f. [*Text*, p. 68; *Daily Practice*, p. 73].
52. HAASE (see note 15), p. 113. [*Text*, p. 86; *Daily Practice*, p. 93].
53. RICHTER (see note 49), p. 24. [*Text*, p. 69; *Daily Practice*, p. 74].
54. Pierre Bourdieu et al., *Un art moyen: Essai sur les usages sociaux de la photographie*, 2d ed. (Paris: Éditions de minuit, 1965), p. 113. [Translated by Shaun Whiteside as *Photography: A Middle-brow Art* (Cambridge, England: Polity Press, 1990), p. 77].
55. SAGER (see note 9), p. 16. [*Text*, p. 62; *Daily Practice*, p. 66].
56. SAGER (see note 9), p. 27. [*Text*, p. 63; *Daily Practice*, p. 68].
57. Catalogue from Galerie h (see note 21), p. 29 f. [*Text*, p. 42; *Daily Practice*, pp. 47-48].
58. RICHTER (see note 22), p. 19. [*Text*, p. 131; *Daily Practice*, p. 141].
59. WARHOL, Andy, *From A to B and Back Again: The Philosophy of Andy Warhol* (New York and London: Harcourt Brace Jovanovich, 1975), p. 149.
60. VAN BRUGGEN (see note 29), p. 86.
61. VAN BRUGGEN (see note 29), p. 86.
62. *Künstler im Gespräch* (see note 7), p. 130. [*Text*, p. 109; *Daily Practice*, p. 117].
63. RICHTER (see note 22), p. 20. [*Text*, p. 133; *Daily Practice*, p. 146].
64. «The paintings are often even kitschy, when I bring all the elements from myself into them, because I'm not just good and rational and all that, but I also put all the rubbish into them.» This quotation, attributed to the artist by van Bruggen (see note 29), p. 91, would have to be checked against the original interview, conducted in German. One wonders whether Richter would have characterized his landscapes from the sixties as «kitschy».
65. RICHTER (see note 22), p. 27. [*Text*, p. 136; *Daily Practice*, p. 146].

«WHERE WE HAVE GOT TO»*

Rainer Rochlitz

The various exchanges between painting and photography have been one of the most striking phenomena of the past few decades in the realm of the visual arts. It is above all through photography that art has reintegrated representation, figuration, the subject and narration. Conversely, it is certain formal aspects of photography which have kindled the interest of painters.

The experiences of painting and the other plastic arts have had repercussions on photography right from its beginnings. But photography belongs only partially to the realm of art. Its documentary functions, whether in the service of individual or collective memory, the press, science, history or even—through the use of identity photographs—the bureaucracy, are quantitatively more significant. In the visual arts, it fulfills several crucial functions, notably that of representing fragments of the real more faithfully and convincingly than, generally speaking, the human hand. Such «representation» however is merely technical; the cognitive value of a less faithful drawing *may* be superior. Which is why the analysis of formal qualities and composition has as important a function for art photography as for drawing or painting.

Right from the beginning, as we now know, photography was used by painters. Some of them simply packed up and switched to

* Passage of Rainer Rochlitz book *L'art au banc d'essai*, Paris: Éditions Gallimard, 1998, chapter III: «Deux artistes».

photography; others continue to paint, but have seemingly adopted the possibilities of photography as their own art's ideal; still others are alternatively painters, sculptors, photographers and videomakers. There is no longer any hierarchical distinction between these different practices. The age-old rivalry between painting and photography has been blurred.

In 1946, in an article on Edward Weston and Walker Evans, Clement Greenberg felt he had to justify photography's naturalist and anecdotal character *by contrast* with the modern taboo imposed upon such characteristics in painting and poetry.[1] The idea of such a taboo was widely shared at the time, but proved to be relatively short lived. All vestiges of «naturalism» were not definitively banned from «all the other arts». Greenberg is actually not far from contradicting himself. Once again in 1946, he argued that though Edward Hopper was of course «not a painter in the full sense», his painting was «essentially photography, and... literary in the way that the best photography is.» But he concluded that «if he were a better painter, he would, most likely, not be so superior an artist.»[2] It is thus possible, according to Greenberg, to be a good artist even while straying from the beaten track of modernism.

With the work in the field of photography undertaken by Warhol and Richter, Cindy Sherman, Jeff Wall and their successors, photographic «reality» at once acquired an entirely different status and lost its naturalistic, naïve and «transparent» character. For Warhol and Richter, photography's indicial contingency has itself become a pictorial sign, and thus at the same time, from being testimony of factual existence, has become an emblematic sign. For Sherman and Wall—as indicated by Sherman's first titles, *Untitled Film Stills*—the photographic image is denied its *upstream* contingency; their staging of «*tableaux vivants*» is such that the stamp of reality is no longer but a simulacrum of photographic authenticity. The image is utterly fabricated like a landscape or cityscape that has been reconstituted in a studio. When Jeff Wall refers to his works as transparencies, what Greenberg understood by «transparency» is nothing more than an artistic fiction. Here, *transparency* means at once «slide» and «transparent» in the sense of a back-lit panel—a device which has been around since the baroque age.

As a technique, photography is used by many contemporary artists. Richter painstakingly «reproduces» photographs with a brush, including on many occasions amateur photographs. Like a filmmaker, Wall has, with similar fastidiousness, «reconstituted» genre scenes analogous to those found in classical painting, which he then proceeds to photograph and present, neon lit, in «light boxes».

Producing pseudo-photographs in oil on canvas is based upon an inversion of the relationship between painting and photography which can be explained only by the observation that the photographic image has become *the* visual reference of our times, at any rate in the eyes of the broad public for whom contemporary painting concerns only the elites. Painting is able to attract attention to the technical, plastic and even ideological properties of the photographic image, to the «pictorial» heritage which informs it, to the inferred visual habits it elicits. Here photography ceases to function as the stamp of the real and becomes a sign revealing a way of seeing.

When reproduced by a painter, almost identically so to speak, a photograph which was taken without any artistic intention, for instance a family snapshot, undergoes transformation. The photographer is often unable to determine beforehand the elements which appear in his visual field either as a whole or in their spatiality, and, without subsequent manipulation, is unable to hinder the involuntary reproduction of certain amongst them in the shot. On the other hand, when the painter reproduces these same elements, their presence stems from deliberation alone which is so total as to affect the very space in which they are set. In that way, he confers upon them both a meaning and an exemplary value, an emblematic status which attracts the viewer's attention.[3] This value is proper, as a constitutive claim, to the painter's works, whether he reproduces photographs or not. But when he does, the contrast between the two media is all the more salient: the medium of exemplary meaning reduces the testimony from factual existence to its function as pure image.

Sherman's and Wall's «filmmaker-like» photography explores indicial contingency by arranging it in keeping with a preconceived image. In her innumerable roles, behind masks and involving the widest variety of accouterments, Cindy Sherman is herself the actress of her own stagings. But these roles only emphasize the accidental character of her underlying physical «truth»: the fact that the actress Cindy Sherman actually exists and possesses a certain number of physical characteristics is not essential to her photographs. The only thing that counts in her work is the *appearance* of photographic reality.

In Jeff Wall's early work, the image, rather than naively reproducing its object, self-reflexively reveals the photographic device and the implicit play of gazes: that of the photographer, the lens's pseudo-gaze and the more or less stereotypical gaze of the photographed subject. Significantly, however, the complete revelation of the device was reserved for one single work. *Picture for Women* can, of course, be thought of as Wall's manifesto, but the subsequent works renounced showing the device. A revelation of this kind is not even *constitutive* of every work.[4] The characteristics of the photographic image, which are at times discreet, and the dialectic of gazes, often absent, are emphasized by various means.

In the case of both Richter and Wall, the «photographic» work is mediated through a reference to painting—technical in the case of Richter, iconographic in the case of Wall.[5] Documenta X did of course exhibit Richter's photographic *Atlas*—from which he has taken his motifs—as an artwork, but it is doubtful whether Richter needs to be included in the history of photography; it is the non-artistic character of most of the photographs he uses which counts. The same no doubt holds for Jeff Wall: his photographs stem more from a history of art whose techniques and supports can no longer, in the contemporary period, be identified with a particular medium, and his work's references to the history of painting are more significant than its references to the history of photography.

«Contemporary art» is not everything being produced in the contemporary period. One might roughly describe it—independently of any notion of quality—as everything which belongs to a context of artistic inquiry and debate in which the object is to establish a specifically reflexive relationship toward images, and whose vocation is to draw the attention of contemporaries to aspects which they had hitherto overlooked. There is a great variety of such reflexive relationships toward the image, of which none is *a priori* more pertinent or important than the others. But the works of Richter and Wall are assuredly part of this context of inquiry.

The flattening of Duchamp

The object of many of Richter's works is to bring about the transmutation of photographic contingency into an emblematic image, but that is far from being the case for all his work which includes monochromes, abstract paintings, more or less synthetic reproductions of classical paintings, color tables, objects such as the *Vier Glasscheiben (*Four Glass Panels, 1967), mirrors and so on. This diversity challenges the idea according to which every artist develops and inflects an «idea» or a small number of closely linked formal ideas. Arthur Danto lists Richter, along with Sigmar Polke and Rosemarie Trockel, as artists whose every show «looks like a group show».[6] With his «objects less», Michelangelo Pistoletto provided an early prefiguration of this tendency in the mid sixties; one could also mention Gasiorowski in this regard; «art operators» Yoon Ja & Paul Devantour more recently made a system out of it, inventing the names of fictional artists for themselves. These are all signs of the fact that today the artist does not necessarily identify with a «manner», a recognizable «logo» as was still the case with Buren's stripes. The question then arises as to whether it is still meaningful to talk about Richter's «style» or what actually constitutes the «styles» of the works of artists of this kind.

Criticism has focused on a suggestion by Benjamin Buchloh, who believed he had discovered in this sort of art a «rhetoric of painting», an «inventory» of techniques and possibilities,[7] undertaken in the spirit of a certain type of literary criticism devoted to the analysis of rhetoric rather than to the analysis of the works' content.[8] Richter himself has refused to accept this hypothesis which would have made of him a sort of post-modern theorist, and various critics have sought to justify his refusal.[9] The wanderings of an artist working with such an array of media and genres probably has a somewhat less programmatic explanation. There is a sizable part of uncertainty in any assertion of a credible and plastically convincing orientation of the art of our period.

Analysis in terms of «rhetoric» would render pointless the question as to which of the painter's *works* are important, since they would all have a demonstrative function. An analysis of this kind could satisfy itself with enumerating all the options that have been tried, all the figures deprived of meaning. The art historian's concern is above all to describe and to classify the work's empirical diversity, but he would scarcely be in a position to structure it without at least some kind of a hierarchy as to what are striking, inaugural or consummate works. Critical debate will always seek to understand «minor» works on the basis of those which are «significant». In order to make this distinction, one first has to have grasped what the artist is after—his ambition and line of inquiry—which then enables those works to be discerned in which these objectives are most efficiently, felicitously and deeply accomplished.

Even when carried out with the talent and erudition of Buchloh, there is little sense in examining a work by seeking above all to reconstruct the whole tradition of its art and its place in the history of artistic dead-ends and taboos. To set about studying a work by recalling the history of its genre is perhaps an instructive detour, but it may also be a way of evading the object. A procedure of this kind suggests that the work does not speak for itself, provide the clues necessary for its understanding and is not situated in and of itself in the history reestablished by the specialist. On top of which, the critic suggests that his historical knowledge authorizes him to say what was suitable or inappropriate to do in art at a given moment—when the artist embarked upon the genre in question. In fact, all he really does is to ratify *a posteriori* the choices of those artists who count in his eyes. Instead of understanding the work's properties, internal organization, its more or less clearly marked ambition, interest and strength, a historical and normative analysis of this kind subjects art to the constraints of an ideology critique which has been established as the guideline of creation.

When one sees *Ema* (*Akt auf einer Treppe* [Nude Descending a Staircase], 1996) or *Vier Glasscheiben*, Duchamps' themes spring immediately to mind, particularly if the two works are juxtaposed with one another. There truly seems to be something demystifying about these references in Richter's work. Duchamps' mechanical figure, its movement broken down into successive phases, has been turned into a full-length frontal portrait of the painter's nude wife gracefully descending a wide staircase, discreetly averting her gaze. Based on a photograph taken by the artist himself, skillfully reproducing the photographic blur, this painted image replaces the turn-of-the-century human mechanization with an intimate picture without the slightest irony, which in many ways defies the norms of the avant-garde movements. From this point of view, Richter seems to have gone from Duchamp to a more classical form of representation, or even to Eugène Carrière's symbolist blur.

As compared to Duchamp, *Vier Glasscheiben* radically flattens the *Grand Verre* (Large Glass) of *La Mariée*. One could even see it as a hyper-Duchampian version of the «Glass», this time of ready-made, industrial quality, without the stained-glass painting, without the mechanical Maiden and servant knights. The windows shown do not «mince matters»; the panels of glass are framed and laterally attached to the uprights, so they can be tipped at different angles. None of them being placed upright, the reflective nature and the slight opacity of the glass is made evident. The viewer can walk around these windows which reveal nothing but themselves, their transparency, their slight reflection, their «emptiness» for whomever seeks a «representation» in the window-painting, and above all their diversely inclined frames—like wings in suspension—which vary from show to show as can be seen in the photographs of different exhibitions. Attention focuses henceforth on the panels' very plurality and the variety of their positions.

In the same spirit, *Ema* could be interpreted as something

other than a «return» to a pre-Duchampian situation. Like the *Vier Glasscheiben* with regard to the *Grand Verre*, it could be considered a dedramatization or banalization. If the point is to show a nude descending a staircase, one might as well do so once again «without mincing matters», frontally and in photographic quality. Benjamin Buchloh provides another explanation still: «Richter seems to have understood that the provocative actions aiming at the destruction of a genre and the abandonment of techniques, would, in the post-war period, inevitably bring about the opposite result: that is, the spectacularization of the avant-gardist gesture of critical negation. And it is in this turnaround, at the very moment where the gesture marking the body's imprint and the indicial inscription of the trace as a radical negation of all specularity becomes the spectacular object that the appearance of conservative opposition in Richter's work takes on an unexpected dimension of critical resistance.»[10] But Buchloh has no proof whatsoever of any such critical reflection on the artist's part concerning the excessively «spectacular» character of the neo-avant-garde movements[11]—a reflection which belongs, rather, to the critic himself.

By further banalizing the nude and the stained glass, Richter further undermines his art's raison d'être. The question is henceforth to know what point there is in still painting nudes or making «stained glass». Richter has actually acknowledged on several occasions the predicament in which he finds himself in continuing to paint. A fact to which his shade testers, gray paintings, equally gray mirrors, his patient work as a copyist of photographs which are as banal as possible all testify. His art is vulnerable to nihilism and self-derision. A further example provides the proof.

In 1971, there cannot have been many people outside art circles—in other words, several hundred initiates—who were familiar with the names of Richter and his friend Palermo. Yet that was the year the artist chose to sculpt first in plaster and then in bronze his head and that of his friend, using a very realistic style, the faces being based upon casting. These two perfectly banal male heads were placed face to face on two plinth-columns some five and a half feet high. As the plaster had initially been painted gray, Buchloh felt he could speak of a «hybrid genre situated somewhere between ready-made and painting, sculpture and photographic imprint.»[12] But this reference to the ready-made and black-and-white photography seems forced. It seeks to legitimate a work, which, without these references, is in danger of appearing traditional. According to a stylistic figure of critics who draw their inspiration from Rosalind Krauss, the use of «indicial» techniques is supposed to guarantee in and of itself the intensely contemporary character of the work in the era of late modernity. Certainly, in the case of his pseudo-photographic paintings, the artist begins with a fastidiously reproduced model, but the technique and the effect have nothing to do with those of photography.

Actually this type of work belongs to a genre of classical sculpture and is normally reserved for celebrities and famous artists. Given the status of the two characters and of their aesthetic convictions, the outcome can scarcely be anything but a highly ambiguous work claiming eternal glory for two unknown artists, sure of their talent, but somewhat foreign to the type of celebration typical of the genre. Though Buchloh simply states that the project is «far from all parody»,[13] the work nevertheless recalls the hoax-happening Richter was involved with in 1963 along with Konrad Lueg Fischer: the two of them sat perched on pedestals in a demonstration in favor of «capitalist realism». Over the course of an evening, the exhibition offered viewers «the spectacle of a furniture house and everything it contained as well as, in a special room, the white pedestals on which the artists were perched.»[14]

The ambiguity, however, remains. The second degree is never gratuitous; and, moreover, fame was to catch up with the artist and his sculpture would end up becoming almost serious. In the same way, the pseudo-Duchampian nude would delight the average viewer who, after all, would see it as a figurative painting of perfect contours—and Richter has even said he accepts this reading. His work manifestly plays on several different levels, but it cannot win out every time. Because of its hieratism of a different era, *Zwei Skulpturen für einen Raum von Palermo* (Two Sculptures for a Room by Palermo) can hardly be taken fully seriously as nineteenth-century salon sculpture; but nor does it provoke laughter the way the demonstration in favor of capitalist realism did. It is not, as Buchloh again claimed from the perspective of ideology critique, «the artist as a fascist or socialist realist», taking «the inevitable and necessary first step toward a thorough work on memory»[15]—as if the artist's point were to accomplish a critical staging of totalitarian art. It could be a work which wavers between a Warhol-like cult of the self and a nihilist or dadaist form of self-derision. Richter's works often have this «impossible» aspect: the nude and the portrait of the artist in plaster or bronze are genres of another era and lead to a feeling of uneasiness because they are obviously something else again. Pseudo-photographic painting, which also makes one uneasy, is just as archaic, inasmuch as the oil-on-canvas «reproduction» of what can be instantly grasped by photography is at once a retrograde and somewhat absurd gesture.

When different interpretations oppose one another as they do here, leading at the same time to variable evaluations, what is at issue is not so much contradictory preferences as above all divergent methodological premises. Different readings do not, however, confront us with an irreducible «discrepancy» [*différend*] between points of view. Certain interpretations, charged with prejudices and weighty presuppositions, fail to stand up to an attentive examination of the work; others are not, in the last analysis, incompatible with one another. Not that argumentation can decide unilaterally between different points of view; but it can foster the progression of analysis toward a more just appreciation of the work. What is of still greater importance is that the different interpretations never *aim* at a purely personal reading. Even if inquiry may lead to contradiction, the different lines of inquiry all attempt to understand the work and its importance as *well* as possible, and thus have common objectives. This is, along with the strength of shared cultural norms, the rational explanation of the fact that extreme discrepancies are rare as far as the importance attributed to the different artists of a given period is concerned.

Seeing a genre

Whether dealing with media-based material or some type of message, whether stemming from the everyday or the artistic, what characterizes all Richter's motifs and pretexts is that they are treated at the same time as exemplary of a genre in which the consciousness of their mediatized nature is still absent. It is the painter who makes them exemplary or transforms them into characteristic representations of a way of representing and signifying.

If in Richter's work there is a dialectic of gazes and an interaction with the receptor, it is by means of this generic treatment: the spectator is asked to see not merely the individual image which he has before him but the genre to which it belongs as well as social character of this mode of representation. He is summoned to consider how images function, in much colder fashion than in pop art where the reproduction of emblematic or media photographs—pictures of stars or of catastrophes—actually reinforce the effectiveness and emotional impact to the detriment of the analysis. What is often most fascinating about Richter's images is the insignificance of their pretext; in this way they draw attention to their generic characteristics.

At this point the question arises as to the «genre» of Richter's own paintings and the *grammatical* or constitutive traits of a plastic work of this kind. They are, of course, paintings in the classical sense, unique works painted in oils with a perfect technique for the imitation of photographic appearance. On the canvas's two-dimensional space, which is always respected, they lay out either an imaginary perspective or an abstract space with or without the suggestion of spatial depth. In the case of pseudo-photographic paintings, the space is usually structured according to the gazes, bodies, activities and accessories of the figures, the places and landscapes which they occupy.

As has already been pointed out, this highly traditional procedure masks an uncertainty as to the ends of painting itself and does not in the last analysis define the works' genre. The proof lies, next to the sculptures and the color tables, in the glass panels and the mirrors—

red, yellow and in other colors as well, but above all gray (1991 and 1992). The figurative paintings, after photographs or after classical paintings (Titian, Friedrich) are but one of the poles of this genre, the other being abstract paintings, shade testers, transparent or reflecting surfaces. Their flat surface, like a sensitive charged object without «conceptual» distancing remains the constant: a more or less empty place, more or less saturated with colored presence, more or less transparent or opaque, more or less filled with forms which are identifiable, meaningful or recognizable by their historical references.

If one wanted to find a literary equivalent of this genre of painting, it would have to be a writer who was at once the author of stories in the traditional sense, of purely sound-based poems, of white or transparent pages, lexical permutations, typographical variations, multiple-column layouts, calligrams and drawings. A work of this kind would not be attributable to any particular literary genre, but would maintain the principle of the page printed on various supports, without ever falling back, for instance, into oral literature. It would be part «of literature», it would stem from the «literature genre»—and equivalents are indeed to be found (Perec).

Every one of Richter's images, whether it be figurative, abstract, reflective or transparent, is thus at the same time a *quasi-image*, a quoted image—mimed, simulated, disowned and hopelessly desired in the same way as his romantic landscapes. The artist seems to fully adhere to only a few rare paintings, notably to the representations of those close to him and of whom he took the photographs himself before painting them (*Ema, Betty*); but he adheres at least partially to all these forms of images, because the uncertainty as to what type of painting to do is primary and the portraits of those close to him provide no definitive solution to this problem. One might almost say that the uncertainty as to the task of painting is Richter's avant-gardist dogma.

The motif of the simulacrum runs through his entire work in which it plays a constitutive role: the imitation by hand of a technique dominated by the eye and by the optico-chemical imprint; the production of unique works simulating a technique of multiple reproduction; the suggestion, by means of oil colors, of the black and white and gray of photography, sometimes even of the washed-out colors of a certain type of color photography; the replica rather than the construction of a perspective space, of a gaze initially oriented by a camera lens, of a staging of his borrowings.

It is a type of painting for which the photographic image is not only the «normal» image of our times, but which, due to its spontaneity free of artistic intentions, teaches us most about ourselves: through a distancing effect, seeing a type of familiar image as a genre provides an incitement to cognition. The painter stages the way in which an image speaks to us and discretely emphasizes his idiom: the blurriness, unsteadiness and shakiness of amateur photography; the manipulative insistence and crass seduction of advertising photography; the abstract idealization of tourist-brochure pictures showing the sea or the mountains; the cerebral stylization of identity photographs depicting famous people in encyclopedias. Even his abstract paintings, seemingly without any model at all, *represent the abstract genre*; moreover, they all bear the generic title «Abstract Painting» (*Abstrakte Bild*) followed by a number. This may still be, however, a systematic, almost theoretical procedure close to the «inventory», «repertory» or «cataloguing» which Buchloh mentioned. Their artistic character actually has to do with other aspects: with the *choice* of meaningful motifs, and no doubt, as the artist admits, with the inexplicable *pleasure* of painting.

In spite of the apparently arbitrary character of the images to be reproduced, the choice of the motif turns out to be difficult.[16] This is because the medium and the genre are not embodied with the same intensity in just any specimen. In the case of amateur photographs, only some possess the unconscious eloquence which makes them apt to become photo-paintings. They must have certain characteristics, certain typical imperfections; they must bear witness to practices, pleasures, lifestyles, utopias which make them into emblems of an involuntary historiography. The well-known *Onkel Rudi* (Uncle Rudi, 1965), cheerful look on his face, clad in the cap and coat of the Wehrmacht, is bound up with this type of historiography. His gaze is imbued with political blindness. The picture's blurriness reproached the gaze of the 1960s for its complicity with a desire to forget, to repress the irreparable. In this way, Richter's works mimic scandalous regressions, of which the bust of the artist is one example, as is the pre-Duchampian nude and the picture—kept in a family photo album—of the soldier parading about in his Nazi uniform. But not all of these scandals point in the same direction; at times, the provocation of the gaze aims at unyielding political consciousness, at other times, at the claim for painting's classical status *against* the avant-garde.

The choice concerns images which reveal an incompleteness, without which pictorial duplication would have nothing to contribute: Richter could not paint a news-report photograph which itself expressed any critical consciousness.[17] The advertisements (*Alfa Romeo*, 1966), pictures of victims from the pages of the newspaper (*Acht Lernschwestern* [Eight Nurse Trainees] 1966), encyclopedia portraits showing the heads of celebrities of the sciences, letters and arts, all stem from the same procedure: means of depiction and representation unaware of their historicity and their generic characteristics; all these images are dated, stereotyped, ignorant of the «habitus» which they embody and whose obtuse rigidity are plain for the eye to see thanks to painting.

The inexplicable pleasure partially has to do with the liberation implied by the possibility of turning a vulgar photograph into a real painting. By objectifying the generic traits, Richter frees himself from his own fascination. He is then able, in principle at any rate, paint anything, any photographed object, provided it possesses a credibility, a representativeness as a photograph: «Deer, planes, kings, secretaries. To have nothing more whatsoever to invent, to forget everything that is understood by painting, color, composition, spatiality—everything one knew and thought. It was no longer the condition of art.»[18] The absurdity, the stupidity of images lacking any style and artistic intention whatsoever confers upon them a power which, in the artist's eyes, is more powerful than the deformations carried out by surrealism or by Bacon.[19]

Nothing suggests that the diversity of the media and genres he has worked with refers, in a Nietzschean sense, to the shimmering of a surface deprived of essence by the decline of metaphysics.[20] Richter is, on the contrary, convinced of the necessity, of the legitimacy of these images whose genres are born spontaneously, whether out of a religious tradition or a daily practice like amateur photography. These media and genres as a whole represent the image reservoir into which we can tap and to which the artist is quite unable to add other forms with anything like the same necessity, the same credibility: the photograph is the «credible»[21] image par excellence, the «cult»[22] image, one might almost say, of our time.

Between the negation of the subject and the historical subject

Not all Richter's hundreds—even thousands—of works[23] have the same intensity. It is for good reason that most critics take only a limited number of them into consideration. His *Eisläuferin* (Skating Girl, 1962), his *Hitler* (1962), his *Faltbarer Trockner* (Foldable Clothes-dryer, 1962), his *Neuschwanstein* (1963) or his *Bombardier* (Bomber, 1963)—pathetic clichés or familiar nightmares—generally speaking leave us indifferent. The quest for the painting able to show us who we are and what our present is all about includes a certain number of «waste products». When the echo of collective conscience is just as important as the eloquence of the medium, the framing and the style, it is difficult to hit home every time. One has to imagine Richter patiently copying the photographic reflections of the contemporary world, waiting for the miracle—the encounter with the emblematic motif—to come about: sometimes it happens, often it does not.

The same goes for the hundreds of *Abstrakte Bilder* (Abstract Paintings), many of which are repetitive, and others repugnant. Multiplication is also the indication of confusion: Richter himself, as we know, has admitted to not knowing what to paint.[24] He tries a lot, fails enormously, always aims for the emblematic image, occasionally achieves it, revels in evoking outdated or even false yet always effective beauty: Friedrich-style romantic landscapes, variations of Titian's *Annunciation*. But what is effective may at the same time be nonsense and refer only to regressive desires.

Richter's abstract paintings are just as heterogeneous as his photo-paintings. The experimental and often playful character of his way of working is particularly manifest in this case. He is without the wealth of graphic means and materials, the black and weird imagination borrowed from fairy-tale illustrations, from design and advertising, from archive photos, caricature, and all the images in the world, deployed, for instance, by his friend Polke. Those of Richter's canvases which do not belong to the category of photo-paintings generally remain free of any figurative element. The origins of this abstraction can be surmised right from the very first work acknowledged by the artist in his *Catalogue raisonné 1962-1993*: it stems from the covering over of pseudo-photographic images with brush strokes or daubs which erase the technique of photographic illusion and accentuate the work's surface and pictoriality. It is the contrary of the artificial «blur» which modulates the degrees of simulated photographic precision. The pictorial gesture affirms its freedom with regard to the representative serfdom with which it has saddled itself elsewhere and which is free only in terms of the choice of its subjects. The full range of techniques for applying paint are then employed to create pictorial spaces which are opposed to the flattened-out spaces of photographic reproduction. These spaces go from the virtual, naively sidereal landscape (*Abstrake Bild*, 1977 [422]), to thickly applied paint that has been scratched or even scraped at, then covered over by means of various instruments, loud colors, reminiscent of expressionism, or faded colors, bordering on monochromes, via gray opacities and strangely transparent frost patterns (*Januar*, 1989 [699], *Eis*, 1989 [706-2]). From photographic representation to the absolute non-representation of the pictorial matter, via the transparent glass and the mirror, all manners of affecting a flat surface are matters for painting.

Compared with Warhol's serigraphs such as *Small Race Riot* (1964) or *Big Electric Chair* (1967), the subjects of Richter's photo-paintings are usually of only provincial interest. Like Warhol, but in less spectacular fashion, he of course also evokes the irruption of violent death (*Tote*, 1963 [9], *Acht Lernschwestern*, 1966 [130], the series *18. October 1977*, 1988), but without dramatizing the news item.

The strength of his way of working consists in using amateur photographs or documents which catch their motif red-handed, as it were, in the midst of existence, as for instance in *Sekretärin* (Secretary, 1964 [14]), one of his oils in black and white. Appearing furtively as she moves down an office hallway, cut off at shin level, the young woman is brightly lit, no doubt by neon. Her back, the bottom of her tightly fitting skirt which covers her knees, her hands with the fingers affectedly spread apart, cast their shadow on a closed door bearing an inscription which is indecipherable with the exception of the name «Louise». Her black hair done up, wearing stylish glasses, an intense red lipstick on her pursed lips beneath her pointed nose, a small bolero with alternately vertical and horizontal stripes: her appearance is scrupulous, studiously eroticized; her face slightly blurred, her gaze pensive but alert. This impeccably slim woman is swept along by the whirlwind of her urgent tasks. Her look and the movement of her body betray her identification with the constraints of a role. Painted after an existent photograph, Richter's painting is neither caricature nor denunciation. By selecting this situation, this instant, this person, he focuses attention on a contemporary archetype frozen into a definitive rigidity.

Between the *48 Porträts* (48 Portraits) of 1972 and the *18. Oktober 1977*, a series painted in 1988, Richter doesn't seem to have done any black-and-white photo-painting. Like Warhol in his *Thirteen Most Wanted Men* (1964), he chose to work from police photographs —documents *par excellence* of the violence inherent in any society, in this case a violence founded upon the rejection of past violence. Extremely blurred pictures of dead bodies lying on the ground, the picture of a hanged woman whose shape can barely be seen, softened views of a burial, then of an arrest taking place in the street seen from afar and from a rooftop, pictures of an old electrophone, of a «cell» occupied above all by a bookshelf full of books, but also the pictures of two identifiable women, whose titles—*Gegenüberstellung* (Confrontation) and *Jugendbildnis* (Youth Portrait)—fail to name but which are nevertheless well-known: they are the two principle members of a well-known terrorist group. The second and third of the *Gegenüberstellungen,* in particular, recalls the style of the first photo-paintings: their absence of pose, the movement grasped in the «unsteadiness» of the image, the uncontrolled expression of faces, a provocative smile seen head on, then, in the other picture of the same woman, a depressed profile, a downward-looking gaze. These images' referential power is enormous. But even if we knew nothing of the fate of these two young women, the black and white and the blur against a neutral background would have dramatic power; the first images, showing the dead, in any case set the tone for the rest of the series. In his greatest series of photo-paintings, Richter painted the documents of a historical mess, brought on tragically by the adjournment of the work of memory. These paintings are a response to the scandal designated by *Onkel Rudi;* some fifteen years before the drama, Richter had experienced an analogous revolt and had recorded it in a painting literally grating with powerlessness. Ten years after the 1977 drama, he once again painted the scenes that everyone would have preferred to forget.

Several months after the *18. Oktober 1977* cycle, Richter painted a series of «glaciations»: *Grat, Januar, Dezember, November, Eis,* which are no doubt amongst his greatest «abstract» paintings. The titles refer to concrete representations, to a discolored and barren nature, and to frost patterns. One seems to recognize stalactites, layers of ice on windows, somber glaciers—but they are nothing but abstract forms. These works are free of any pretense of «total freedom» and explosive colors. An all-over technique resorts to a great variety of traces; little streaks, touches, impressions, drips of bright colors are lost in the black, the white, the dirty gray. There is no dead space; all the surfaces are integrally animated and intense. Richter even succeeds in convincing us that certain spots are «blurred» (the bright colors in the lower part of *Eis,* 1989 [706-2]), whereas other spots (in the middle center) seem «sharp». The glacier-like masses crumble away or become leprous. The surfaces become worn, scratched, spattered, as if dogged by chance. All of which only ends up intensifying their second life. They are ultimately delicate and subtle.

Though some of Richter's paintings done after photographs, such as the portrait of his daughter (*Betty*, 1988 [663-5]), reproduce «poses», all narration is absent. This young woman is of the same age as the *Jugendbildnis* of one of the prisoners painted the same year. Her lost profile seen against a somber background refers less to any suggestion of the relationship between the artist and his model than to the negation of a convention of photographic portraiture, whose objective it is to reproduce the face. The pseudo-photographic accuracy of the shoulder and hair takes the place of focusing on the face. The picture's interest shifts toward the finesse of her blond hair done up in a bun, its highlights more or less brought out by the light, and above all toward her clothes, a hooded wool jacket—white with red-flower colors—worn over a red sweater: children's garments, at once warm and of a forced cheerfulness. The painter's daughter seems to flee her father's gaze as he envelopes her in adolescence, denying her nascent womanhood.

The eloquence of these paintings is indirect. Why *Betty* has become one of the painter's emblematic works is not immediately obvious. The image is «beautiful» just as some of the painter's landscapes—at the limit of the facile—are «beautiful»; its beauty is due to the youthfulness suggested by the flesh tints of the neck and jaw, the hair's freshness, the merry childishness of her clothing. Seen from the front, the portrait of the young girl would scarcely have produced an exemplary work. The refusal of the face gives the work its «contemporary» character. It refers to a certain impossibility of the naïve portrait.[25] However, *Betty* is not modern in the sense that a Bacon portrait is, with its violent deformations. Here as elsewhere, Richter helps himself to beauty. But painting after a photograph, he once again needed an image which was incomplete, frozen in conventional representative practice. In this case, however, he did not start with a stereotypical amateur photograph, but rather with a snapshot based upon a pose before the artist. The image's emblematic character, its «grace», like that of *Ema* (1966 [134])—the «nude descending a staircase»—undoubtedly has to do with the complicity, the love binding the artist to his model, which suppresses the non-meaning inherent in most of his photo-paintings. But these few exceptions, which in some respect glorify intimate life, only serve to emphasize the emptiness of meaning and the stereotypical character of the great majority of his subjects.

In the existent images of private or common memory, in family snapshots or archive images of a terrorist group in prison, Richter seeks characteristics which testify to their quality as images of a significant state of collective consciousness. His works' interest lies not in a critical or ironic intention, or in a refusal to tow the line, but rather, in keeping with a fairly classical conception of the painter's task, and from the various angles of one complex sign, in a quest for the emblematic image. He seeks to explain, by means of the image, the «point where we have got to»,[26] not according to any sociological analysis, but according to historical experience. These different poles are opacity and transparency with all their intermediary gradations; genres defined by their social function; and finally, their real reference to a fragment of reality, a well-known painting, an advertisement, an historical event. All these aspects make up what the artist refers to by the traditional term of «appearance».[27] Like him, though in an assuredly more sulfurous fashion, Warhol reproduced and monumentalized existent photographs, logos and effigies; like him, Lichtenstein simulated, fabricated and parodied pictorial gestures.[28] But few artists have covered the field of the visible as exhaustively as Richter has, in search of the eloquent image.

The difficulty thus consists in discovering the common procedure between the photo-paintings—which are meditations on history—and the formal studies, variations on classical paintings, color tables, gray mirrors, abstract paintings and objects such as sculpted heads and glass panels. The exploration of a vast formal repertory seems to be a sign both of confusion as to art's function and of a taste for experimentation.

This analysis reveals the opposition between two interpretations. One, over-politicized, justifies the work on the basis of a certain number of artistically correct references: the *a priori* value of the indicial principle of photography or the critical interest in a rhetorical inventory of painting. The other endeavors to understand Richter's experiences in an immanent fashion, like a quest for the emblematic image and a challenge for the impossible and scandalously archaic image, forever charged with impregnable emotions. The great diversity of works and their considerable number inevitably requires a very different style of analysis than would the analysis of novels. Each painting is like a poem isolated from its collection; and it is only the knowledge of the series, even of entire categories of works, which allows one to grasp the meaning of what the artist is after.

Notes:

1. GREENBERG, Clement, «The Camera's Glass Eye: Review of an Exhibition of Edward Weston» (*The Nation*, 1946), in *Clement Greenberg. The Collected Essays and Criticism*, vol. 2, *Arrogant Purpose, 1945-1949*, ed. by John O'Brian (Chicago and London: University of Chicago Press, 1986), p. 61: «Modern painting has had to reduce its ostensible subject matter to the impersonal still life or landscape, or else become abstract, for a number of reasons, historical, social, and internal, that hardly touch photography in its present stage. Photography, on the other hand, has at this moment an advantage over almost all the other arts of which it generally still fails to avail itself in the right way. Because of its superior transparency and its youth, it has, to start with, a detached approach that in the other modern arts must be struggled for with great effort and under the compulsion to exclude irrelevant reminiscences of their pasts. Photography is the only art that can still afford to be naturalistic and that, in fact, achieves its maximum effect through naturalism. Unlike painting and poetry, it can put all emphasis on an explicit subject, anecdote, or message; the artist is permitted, in what is still so relatively mechanical and neutral a medium, to identify the "human interest" of his subject as he cannot in any of the other arts without falling into banality.»
2. GREENBERG, «Review of the Whitney Annual» (*The Nation*, 1946), in ibid., p. 118.
3. RICHTER, Gerhard, *Text* (Frankfurt am Main: Insel, 1993), p. 29, distinguishes, in this sense, between the mere «seeing» of the photographer and the «knowing» of the drawer.
4. This is doubtless why Thierry de Duve attempts to bring out *another* of Wall's techniques, intended to provide the photographic image with *modern* painting's self-reflexive character (the reference being to Cézanne's convex space). But this technique which is problematic to bring out and whose function somewhat unclear, is not

constitutive of his work as a whole. See Thierry de Duve, Arielle Pelenc, Boris Groys, eds., *Jeff Wall* (London: Phaidon Press, 1996), pp. 34 *sq*.

5. This is also the case for the «genre photographer» Thomas Struth, disciple of Bernd and Hilla Becher.

6. DANTO, Arthur, *Embodied Meanings. Critical Essays and Aesthetic Meditations* (Farrar, Straus & Giroux: New York, 1994), p. 333.

7. BUCHLOH, Benjamin, *Gerhard Richter. Essais* (Paris: Éditions des Musées de la Ville de Paris), 1993, p. 105.

8. Buchloh undoubtedly had Paul de Man in mind.

9. See Gertrud Koch, Luc Lang, Jean-Philippe Antoine, *Gerhard Richter*, trans. by Brian Holmes (Paris: Dis Voir, 1995), pp. 21, 24 and 26. To this sort of irony, Gertrud Koch opposes a «tragic» dimension, conflictual thought, the painting of the veils of the Revelation, fallen metaphysics; pp. 51 *sq*. Luc Lang argues that «in this way, Richter relentlessly tests painting's capacity to *tolerate* a world of ever more universal and planetary image-based media».

10. BUCHLOH, op. cit., p. 24.

11. In 1964 Beuys stated that «Marcel Duchamps' silence is overestimated.» Without being a Beuysian, Richter was nonetheless attentive to his work and may have supported this reevaluation of the Duchampian avant-garde and wanted to «demystify» Duchamps' exemplary works.

12. BUCHLOH, op. cit., p. 29.

13. Ibid., p. 31.

14. Ibid., p. 72.

15. Ibid., p. 32.

16. RICHTER, op. cit., p. 32; BUCHLOH, op. cit., p. 96. In an interview, the artist stated: «No, the motifs were never fortuitous, I went to far too much trouble to find the odd picture I could use».

17. For another type of incompleteness—aesthetic in this case—required for Fernand Léger's subjects, see Rainer Rochlitz, «La "matière première" de Fernand Léger», in catalogue *Fernand Léger* (Paris: Éditions du Centre Georges Pompidou, 1997).

18. RICHTER, op. cit., p. 28.

19. Ibid., p. 32.

20. Gertrud Koch's interpretation in Koch, *et al.*, op. cit., p. 26.

21. RICHTER, op. cit., pp. 25, 31.

22. Ibid., p. 25.

23. In 1993, the *Catalogue Raisonné* enumerated 794 entries, some of which are made up of many paintings—and the production continues.

24. RICHTER, op. cit., pp. 76, 85, 114, p. 162 *sq*., 199.

25. Two other *Bettys* are dated 1977 (425-4, 425-5). The first work shows the young woman horizontally, the second is blurry to the extent of making identification impossible.

26. RICHTER, op. cit., pp. 80, 85, 87, 146, 206.
27. Ibid., p. 171.
28. Some of his «strokes» are so broad that no paintbrush in the world would be able to paint them (*Strich*, 1979 [451, 452]).

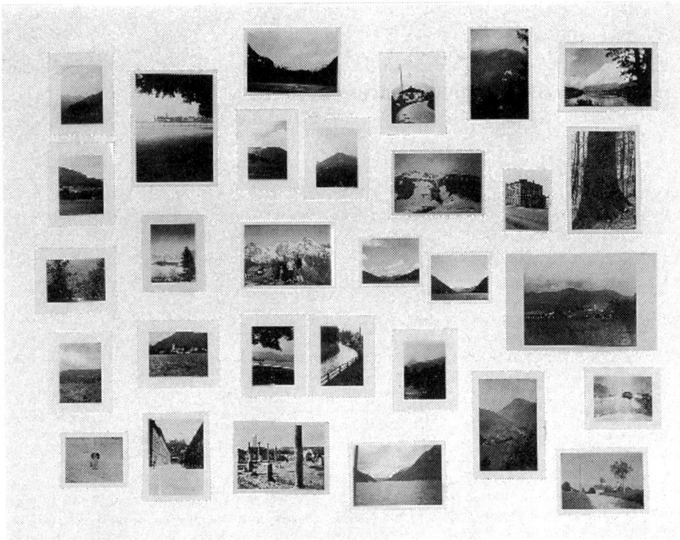

Atlas, 4: *Albumfotos* (Album photographs), 1962-1966

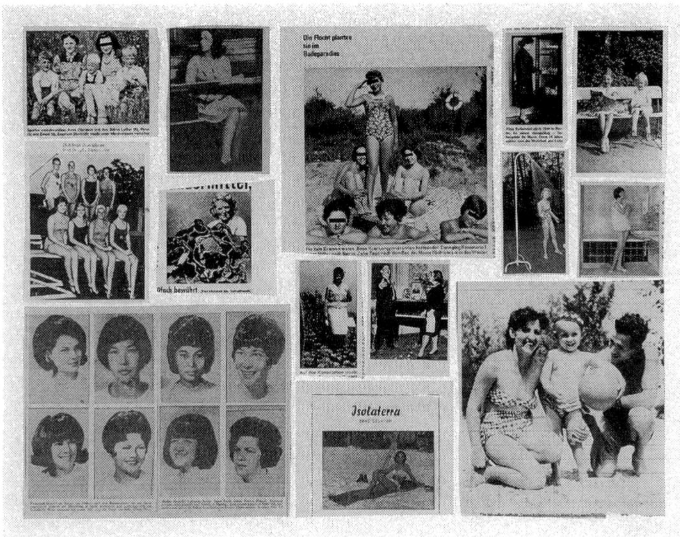

Atlas, **8**: *Zeitungsfotos* (Newspaper photographs), 1962-1966

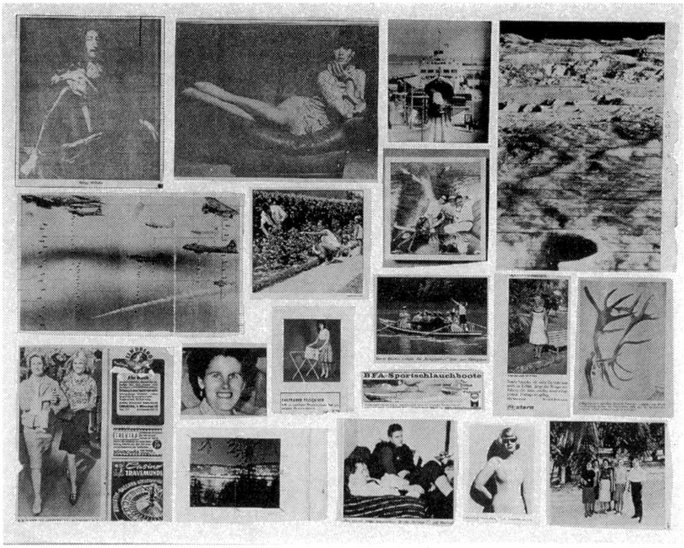

Atlas, **10:** *Zeitungsfotos* (Newspaper photographs), 1962-1968

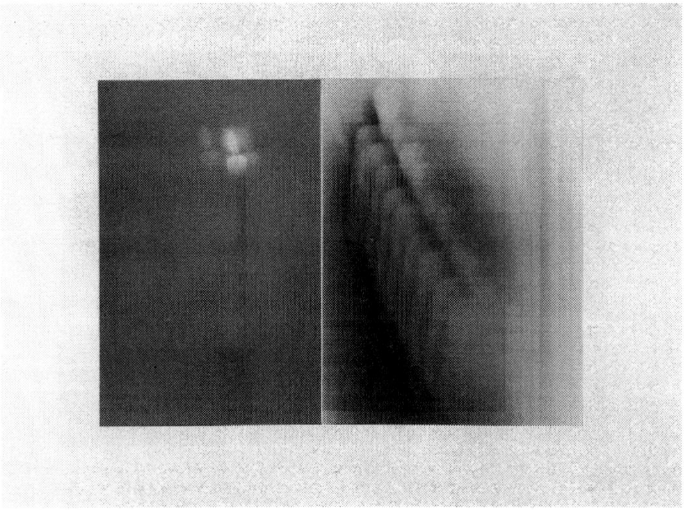

Atlas, **68:** *Fotos* (Photographs), 1969

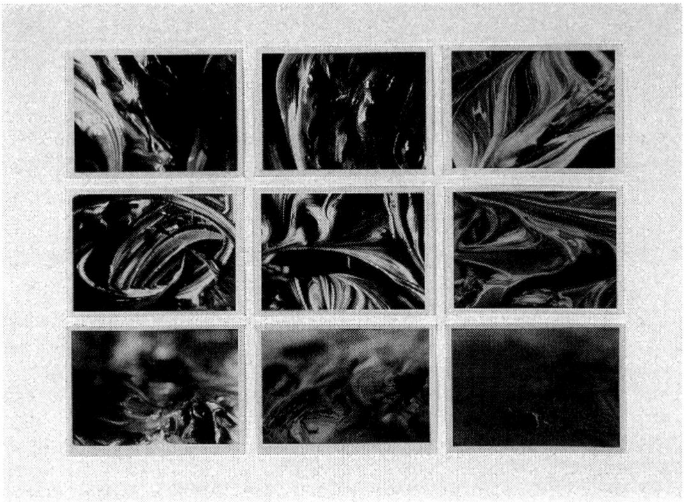

Atlas, **93**: *Ausschnittfotos* (Photograph Sections), 1970

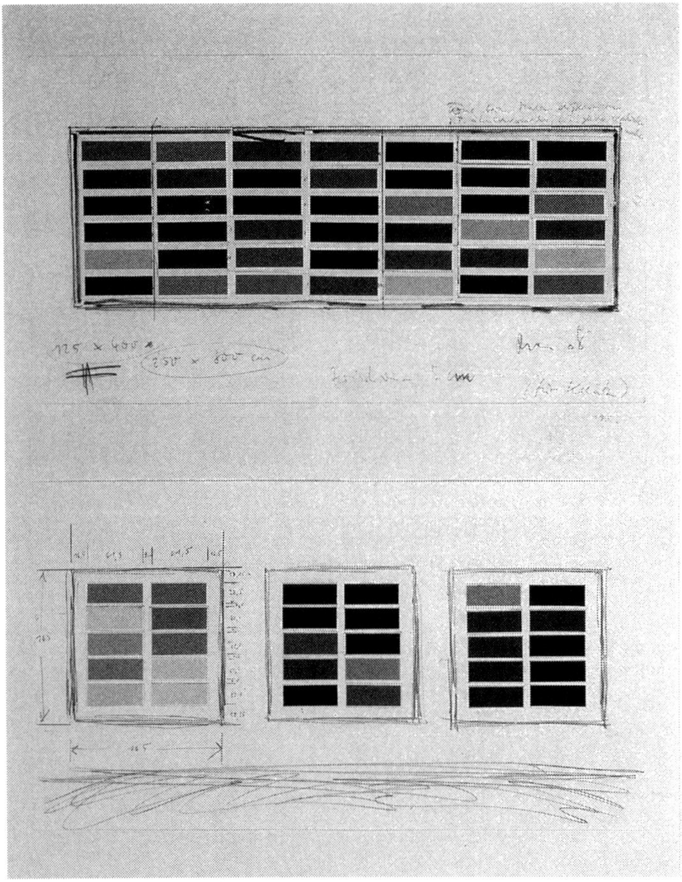

Atlas, **278:** *Farbtafeln* (Colour Tables), 1966

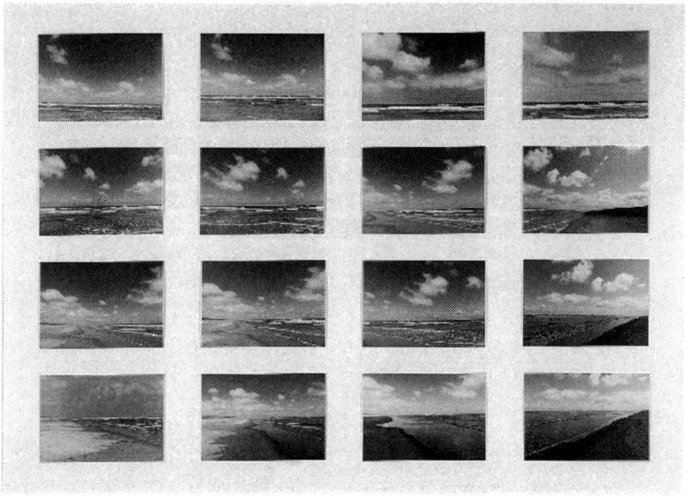

Atlas, **323**: *Seestücke* (Seascapes), 1975

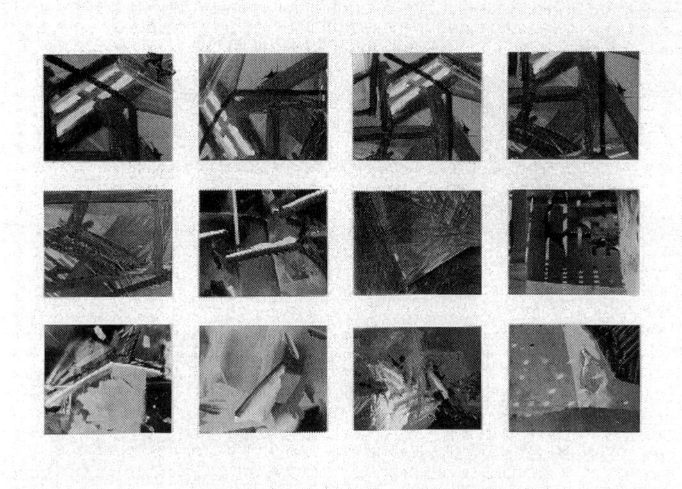

Atlas, 412: *Abstrakte Bilder* (Abstract Painting), 1977

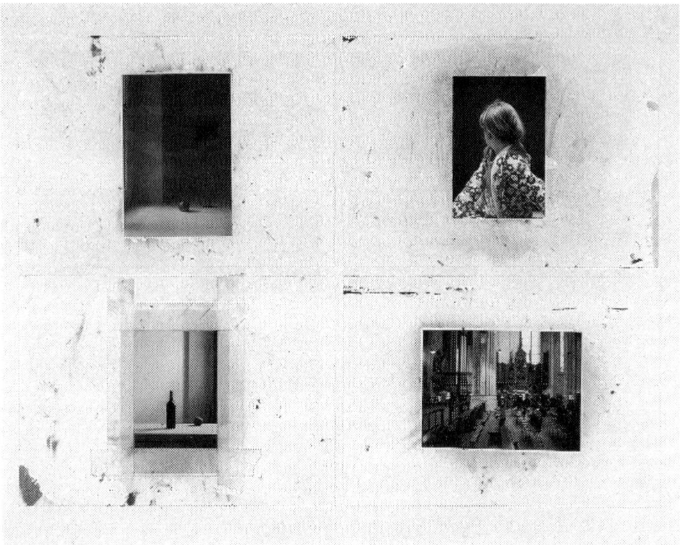

Atlas, 445: *Verschiedene Motive* (Various Subjects), 1978/1984/1988

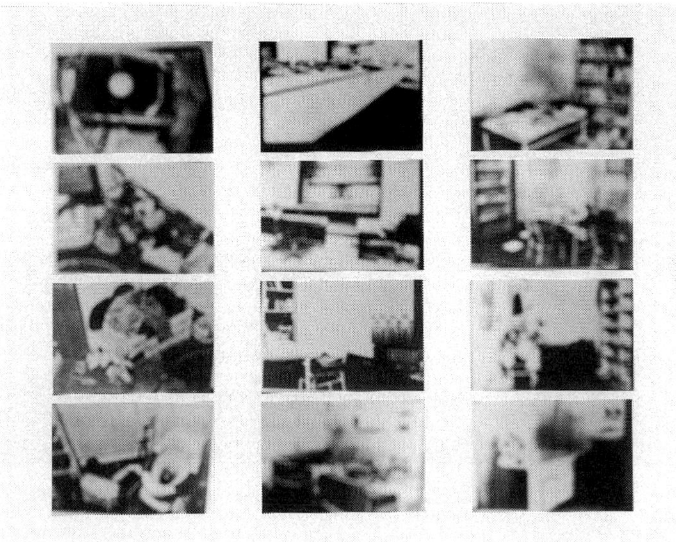

Atlas, 478: *Baader-Meinhof-Fotos* (Baader-Meinhof photographs), 1989

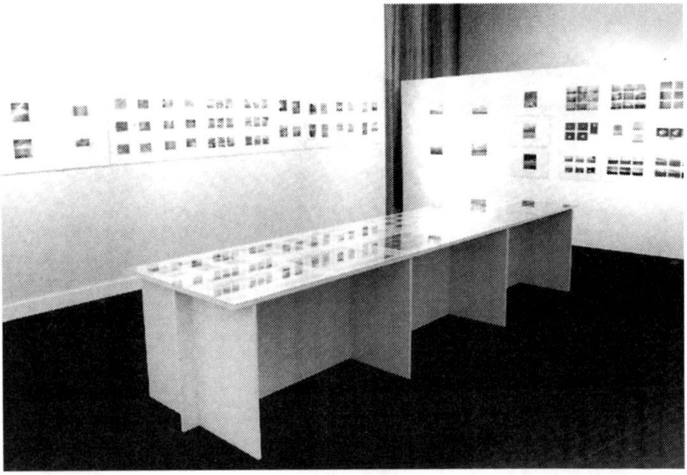

View of the first installation of the *Atlas*, Hedendaagse Kunst, Utrecht, December 1972.

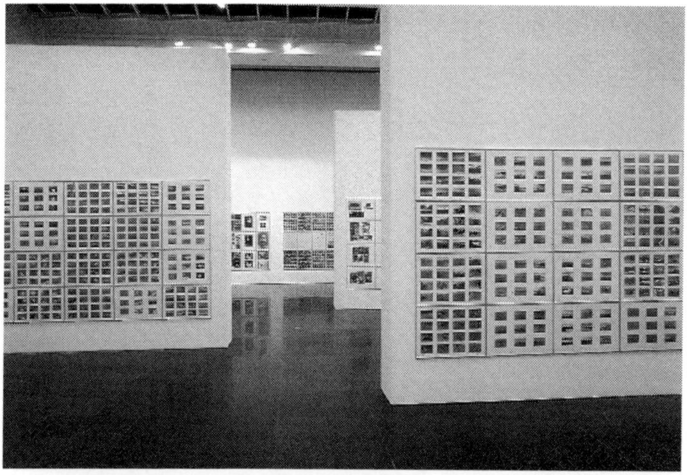

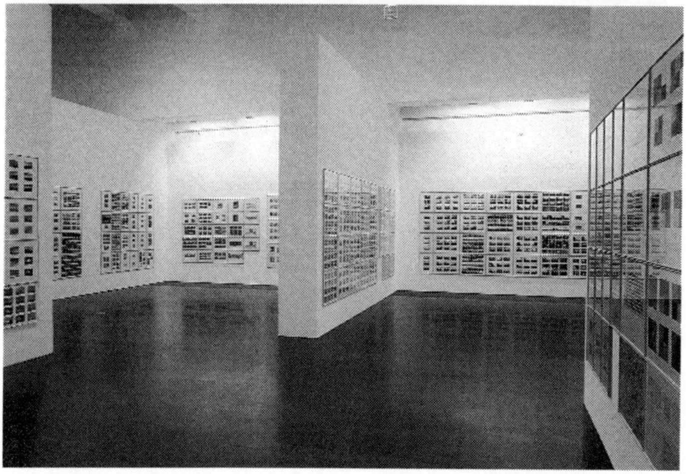

Views of the installation at MACBA, Barcelona, April-July1999